DUPLEIX

Owing to the antiquity and rarity of this book, certain pages are regrettably absent, and readability is compromised due to the blurring of the original text. If you possess any insights regarding the availability of these missing sections, kindly inform us. Your assistance is crucial in ensuring the completion of this significant work for the benefit of future generations.

DUPLEIX

AND THE STRUGGLE FOR INDIA BY THE EUROPEAN NATIONS

GEORGE BRUCE MALLESON

GYAN

Published by

GYAN

Gyan Publishing House
5, Ansari Road
Daryaganj, New Delhi-110002
Phone: 011-47034999, 9811692060
E-mail: books@gyanbooks.com

Distribution Network
gyanbooks.com
India, USA, Canada, UK, Australia

ISBN: 978-93-7097-381-7 (PB)
First Published, 1899

2nd Impression 2025

Printed at: Gyan Press, Delhi.

DUPLEIX
Arthur GEORGE BRUCE MALLESON

RULERS OF INDIA

EDITED BY

SIR WILLIAM WILSON HUNTER

DUPLEIX

AND THE STRUGGLE FOR INDIA BY THE EUROPEAN NATIONS

BY

COLONEL G. B. MALLESON, C.S.I.

OXFORD

AT THE CLARENDON PRESS

CONTENTS

NOTE

I have to acknowledge the obligations under which I am to the under-mentioned writers: (1) Orme's *History of India*; (2) Cambridge's *Account of the War in India,* containing the Journal of Colonel Stringer Lawrence; (3) The Abbé Guyon's *History of the East Indies,* 1757; (4) The Memoirs of Dupleix, and of Labourdonnais, and a contemporary Memoir of Lally; (5) Laude's *Le Siège de Pondichery en* 1748, containing the Journal of Rangapoulé; and many modern works. I have also with me information which I gathered from Pondichery and Chandarnagar, relating to the events here recorded, during my service in India.

DUPLEIX

CHAPTER I

INTRODUCTORY

'THE immense riches,' wrote the Abbé Guyon in 1774, 'which the Portuguese, the English, and the Dutch had drawn from the East Indies, invited the French to follow them in those remote and unknown countries, in order to partake of the advantages of which commerce was there productive.' For many years, indeed, the 'invitation,' as the Abbé calls it, had dangled before the French people. For many years they had failed successfully to respond to it. In vain had Francis I in 1537 and 1543, and Henry III in 1578, exhorted their subjects to make long voyages. As these exhortations were unaccompanied by any promise of a State subsidy, as had been similar offers in the three countries which preceded France in the race for the commerce of the East, they produced no effect whatever. Nor was it till 1615 that a Company, which four years previously had obtained from Louis XIII letters patent for the monopoly of the Eastern trade for twelve years, stimulated by two merchants of Rouen, MM. Muisson and Canis, made a beginning by despatching two vessels to the Indian Ocean.

The vessels equipped and despatched by this Company touched indeed at Madagascar, but did not touch India. But the account they brought home of the riches of Madagascar stimulated to a certain extent the spirit of enterprise among the public, and to a still greater degree in the ruling circle, then directed by the illustrious Richelieu. On the 24th of June, 1642, that eminent statesman granted to a new Company the exclusive privilege of settling colonies in Madagascar and the adjacent islands, and taking possession of them in the name of the King of France. Richelieu died in December of the same year, and Louis XIII in May of the year following. But the idea had taken root, and on the 20th of September, 1643, the Council of Regency confirmed the privileges of the new Company.

Its success was but moderate. The Company did indeed effect a settlement on Madagascar, and every year of its existence it despatched thither at least one well-freighted trading vessel. For a time the proprietors hoped. The arrival of one ship laden with yellow sandal-wood, hides, aloe-wood, and gums, and of another bringing twenty-five tons of rock-crystal, kept up their spirits. But these were only transient successes, which were far from counter-balancing the losses sustained by wrecks and the insalubrity of the climate. When, therefore, the twenty years for which exclusive rights had been granted to it expired, the Company did not ask for a renewal of its privileges.

Its place, however, was at once occupied by a famous nobleman, who had won by his services in the field a dukedom and the bâton of a Marshal of France. This was the Duke de la Meilleraye. He threw into the scheme all the ardour of his nature, but without success, and when he died in February, 1664, after ten years of commercial enterprise, he left behind him a record of failure.

At this crisis France was well served by the statesman whom Mazarin, in his dying moments[1], had recommended to Louis XIV as his successor. The fertile mind of Colbert recognised not only the advantage but the necessity of pushing colonial enterprise. He had noticed with the deepest interest the success of England, Holland, and Portugal in that field. Why, he asked himself, should France fail where those powers had shown that it required but good direction to ensure success? In 1664, then, the very year that the death of the Duke de la Meilleraye had left the field open, he constituted a Company with a capital of fifteen million francs and a concession for exclusive trading for fifty years. So far he followed, on a larger scale, the lines on which his predecessors had marched. But his genius recognised that something more was necessary. He saw that the preceding French companies had failed because they had not

[1] 'Sire, je vous dois tout; mais je crois m'acquitter en quelque sorte envers votre Majesté en lui donnant Colbert.'

had the backing which had made the success of the rivals of France. He therefore, to insure them against the losses which unless provided for might dishearten the proprietors, conceded to the Company an advance of three millions of francs, and charged the State with all the losses it might suffer during the first ten years of its existence. In order, moreover, to induce the nobility to participate in the scheme, Louis XIV, at the instance of his minister, issued an edict declaring that it was not derogatory to the nobility to take part in commerce with the Indies. That, moreover, he might the more certainly obtain the necessary subscriptions, Colbert inserted a clause in the articles by which foreigners were invited to subscribe to the funds of the Company, and were promised letters of naturalisation, free of any formality, provided that any of them should subscribe to the extent of ten thousand francs. Another clause provided that the directors of the Company should be chosen exclusively from the mercantile class, inclusive of foreign merchants, on the conditions regarding the latter, that their money-interest in the Company should be considerable, and that they and their families should reside in France. The statutes of the Company are forty-seven in number. They assure to the Company full power and jurisdiction over Madagascar and all the territories its servants might conquer or occupy, and they contain a promise to defend those places against a foreign enemy with all the force of France. The ordinance was dated August, 1664, and was registered in the parliament in September. Before, however, that registration had taken place, the King, on his own authority, had given an order on the royal treasury for three hundred thousand francs, to be paid into the coffers of the Company.

The wise provisions of the Minister met with success. The money came in rapidly, and in March of the following year (1665), four ships of the new Company, partly armed as ships of war, and carrying 520 men, sailed from Brest for Madagascar. The idea of the Company was to establish on that island a settlement which should serve as a half-way house to India. To this end they offered all sorts of inducements to adventurous natures. They affixed to the walls of the principal cities and towns of France notices wherein they declared that they had resolved to make those who settled in the Colony proprietors of as much land as they, their families, and their servants could till. These notices contained a glowing description of the Île Dauphine—for such was the new name given to Madagascar—stating that the climate was 'very temperate,' that 'two-thirds of the year are like spring;' that 'the other third is not hotter than the summer of France;' that people lived there 'to the age of a hundred, and even of a hundred and twenty;' that 'fruits were good and plentiful;' that there were 'quantities of oxen, cows, goats, hogs, and other cattle;' that there were 'gold, silver, lead, cotton, wax, sugar, tobacco, black and white pepper, ebony, dyeing-wood of all sorts,' and other merchandise; and that it was not even necessary that the settler should himself work to obtain all these things. All that was required of him was to set to work the negroes, 'who are docile, obedient, and submissive,' to gain all that he required. Probably a description more glowing of an island, but one small extremity of which had been explored, was never forced on the attention of any people.

But in spite of these glowing pictures, the colony at Madagascar, as I shall continue to call the island, did not prosper. The adventurers who accepted service under the Company found that the natives, far from being willing to work for them, were actually hostile; that the climate was not only far hotter than that of France, but at certain seasons was actually deadly; that the soil was only moderately fertile; and that many of the richer merchandise promised in the notices existed only in the fertile imaginations of those who had drawn them. After many years of striving against the natives and the climate, the colonists who survived packed up their household goods, and migrated to the neighbouring islands of France and Bourbon, which, discovered and abandoned by the Portuguese, occupied and abandoned by the Dutch, and then nominally taken possession of by France (1649), had remained unoccupied by Europeans until 1672. In that year the baffled colonists of Madagascar, inconsiderable in number, took possession of them, and formed there the nucleus of a settlement which was one day to be powerful.

But the attempts made to colonise Madagascar had not exhausted all the resources of the French Company. Colbert had recognised that the special requirement to ensure success was a man. Hitherto the chiefs of the exploring expeditions had been mere machines. He wanted a man who could think and act for himself, who had a brain to devise and a strong will to execute his daring plans, and who should be, at the same time, patient, laborious, and stedfast. Such a man he believed he had found in 1666 in Francis Caron. Caron, though of French origin, had been born in Holland, and had risen to a high rank in the service of the Dutch East India Company. He was a self-made man who had risen by force of character, and who, on being refused by his masters a post of the highest importance in Batavia, had resigned all his appointments, and tendered his services to Colbert. Colbert accepted them with alacrity, nominated him Director-General of French commerce in India, and despatched him with a new expedition to the Indian seas at the beginning of 1667.

Caron touched at Madagascar. He found the colonists there in a condition so deplorable, that recognising the place to be impossible for the purposes for which it had been originally destined, he did not waste his time there, but pushed on for India. On December 24th of the same year he touched at Cochin, proceeded thence to Surat, and established there the first French factory in India.

Caron had brought with him a Persian called Mercara, in the hope of being able to communicate through him with the native rulers of the adjoining territories. He at once employed Mercara on this service; sent him to the court of the King of Golconda with a request that he might be granted all the trading privileges conceded to foreign nations, and that he might be allowed to establish a settlement at the town of Masulipatam. Whilst Mercara was on this mission Caron busied himself at Surat, and sent thence to Madagascar a valuable cargo. The news of this success was received with enthusiasm in France, and Louis conferred upon Caron the riband of St. Michael.

Meanwhile Caron's agent, Mercara, had obtained all that he asked for at Golconda. He had the usual difficulties to contend with, but his knowledge of the Oriental character enabled him to surmount them, and on December 5, 1669, he obtained a firman which permitted the French Company to trade without import or export duties in the King's dominions, and a license to establish a factory at Masulipatam. Thither Mercara proceeded.

Great as was Caron in many things, he yet possessed one fatal quality—a quality which, it would seem, has deep root in France, for in all her wars no quality has interfered so much with the success which, without it, was attainable. This quality is jealousy of the success of others. Mercara's happy negotiations with the King of Golconda, instead of filling the heart of Caron with joy, aroused only envy. He displayed this feeling in so marked a manner, that, after vainly endeavouring to subdue it, Mercara embarked with his adherents on board a French vessel and sailed to Java. He transmitted at the same time his correspondence with Caron to Colbert, who a little later cleared him from the charges brought against him by Caron.

Meanwhile Caron, great as an organiser, had represented to Colbert that it would be largely to the interests of France if he were allowed to take possession of the island of Ceylon, then partially occupied by the Dutch, to serve at once as a *point d'appui* and a point of departure for French enterprise against India. He told the Minister that his agents had sounded, and had obtained the approval of, the King of Candy to such an expedition. Colbert accepted the idea, and despatched a squadron under Lahaye, a man unfortunately of but mediocre ability, to co-operate with Caron. The two commanders made their first attempt on Point de Gallo in the winter of 1672. But here the Dutch were in force, and the attack was repulsed. The Frenchmen were more fortunate at Trinkámalí, which they took and garrisoned. But hardly had they accomplished this when a Dutch fleet of superior force hove in sight. Lahaye, despairing of success, sailed northward, and whilst the Dutchmen were engaged in recovering Trinkámalí, anchored before St. Thomé, a little settlement near Madras, originally occupied by the Portuguese, but at the moment by the Dutch. Lahaye stormed it with the loss of only five men.

It has ever been the misfortune of the several Governments which have borne sway in France that they have judged almost entirely by results. Into the springs of action of their agent, of the resources at his disposal, of the mode in which he has availed himself of those resources, they are not careful to inquire. The result is what they look at, and if that is unfortunate, the agent is made the scapegoat. Thus it was with Caron. The enterprise against Ceylon, from which so much had been hoped, had failed, for the relieving Dutch fleet had retaken Trinkámalí, and had made prisoners of the garrison. The solitary results of a large expenditure of money and men were the settlement at Masulipatam, won by the dexterity of Mercara, and St. Thomé, of which but little was known. The Directors of the Company urged then on the Minister the recall of Caron. Caron was, not exactly recalled, but ordered in complimentary terms, covering other designs, to return to France. He set out accordingly, and had already passed Gibraltar when he learned from a stray vessel that he was doomed. He altered his course accordingly, and made for Lisbon. But, as he entered the Tagus, his ship struck on a rock, and almost immediately foundered. The only survivor of the disaster was one of the sons of Caron.

The departure of Caron for Europe had left the affairs of the Company in the hands of MM. Lahaye and Baron. To these gentlemen the actual position seemed full of danger. They could scarcely doubt that the Dutch, whose naval preponderance on the coast had enabled them to recover Trinkámalí, would take instant measures to retake St. Thomé. To be provided with a territory, the possession of which no European power could contest, they directed the officer next to them in authority, M. Francis Martin, who had been the trusted lieutenant of Caron, and whose remarkable abilities had conciliated their esteem, to arrange with one of the native princes for the cession of a piece of land on which they might build, and which, fortified with care, might become the head-quarters of the French possessions on the eastern coast of Southern India.

Martin at once entered into negotiations with Sher Khán Lodí, the governor of the possessions of the King of Bíjápur in the Karnátik, and finally was allowed to purchase a plot of land on the sea-coast, in the south Arkát division, comprising an area of 113 square miles, and the districts known as Puducherí, Villanur, and Báhur. The village of Puducherí, which gave its name to the territories, and which, by universal acceptance, is now called Pondichery, was eighty-six miles to the south-south-west of the English settlement of Madras. The purchase concluded and ratified, Martin returned to St. Thomé to report his success to his superiors. He found the place blockaded by the Dutch fleet on the side of the sea, and besieged by the troops of the King of Golconda on the land side. The garrison, 600 strong, defended themselves energetically for some time, but want of provisions soon forced their leaders to treat. The terms they obtained were just such as they wanted. The garrison were allowed to quit the place with all the honours of war, and to proceed whither they might choose. They immediately evacuated the place, and whilst the bulk of them, led by Lahaye and Baron, returned to Surat, some sixty, led by the energetic Martin, proceeded to take possession of the new territory acquired south of the river Coleroon. They reached it in the month of April, 1674.

Thus did Francis Martin found the French India which, a little later, was to contest the supremacy over the entire southern peninsula with the English. He was a man of rare capacity. He knew how to command, how to encourage, how to inspire, how to govern. His first difficulties were great. He and the sixty men with him constituted a small colony of foreigners in a new country, dependent to a great degree on the good-will of the natives, and shut out from all communication with Europe by the Dutch fleet cruising off the coast. The village of Pondichery, where Martin had established his head-quarters, was small, and, as far as accommodation for Europeans was concerned, absolutely destitute. On the other hand, its position left nothing to be desired. It was sheltered against the monsoon, was easy to fortify, extremely healthy, and conveniently situated for mercantile transactions with the interior. Martin's first care was to obtain permission to build accommodation for his men. Fortunately, he had a sufficiency of funds. In his dealings with the natives he displayed a tact which won their confidence and esteem. By degrees the Dutch blockade relaxed, and finally ceased altogether. Then vessels arrived from Europe. A trade in piece-goods was opened with the interior. Despite the wars of the native chiefs, the colony throve rapidly. By-and-by Martin obtained permission to enlist native soldiers for its protection. At the end of two years, he was able to inform the Company that he would send them annually goods to the value of at least 1,000,000 francs.

The year following a crisis came. The famous Sívájí invaded the Karnátik, passed by Madras, took the strong fortress of Gingí, defeated Sher Khán Lodí in a pitched encounter, and threatened to annihilate the French on the pretext that they were allies of Sher Khán. Martin was equal to the occasion. He despatched the valuables of the colonists to Madras, then employed a friendly native chief to represent to Sívájí that he was willing to acknowledge the supremacy of the Maráthás, and to pay for the license to trade. Sívájí accepted his submission, and left him undisturbed. In a few weeks the peril had passed.

It would take too long to record the yearly progress of the little settlement. It must suffice to state that, thanks to the wise measures of the energetic and prudent man who governed it, despite the neglect of the Company at Paris, it prospered. The village was gradually transformed into a handsome town with regular streets. This, too, whilst receiving no increase of Europeans from home. On the contrary, in 1689, the sixty Martin had brought with him had diminished by deaths to thirty-six. Thanks to the permission granted by the son of Sívájí, regular fortifications, laid out it is recorded by a Capuchin monk, were at this period added to the town. The settlement began to be talked about by the sailors who visited the coast as a place of great future promise. Its trade increased. The one thing it required was attention from home.

The reputation it had acquired became at length a cause of peril. In 1693, the Dutch, determined to root out the traders of rival powers, fitted out and despatched to the Indian seas a fleet of nineteen sail of the line, having on board 1,500 infantry besides sailors. It was the most imposing armament which had ever been despatched to India. At the end of August, of the same year, it appeared before Pondichery. The resources of Martin were quite inadequate to meet the threatened attack. He had thirty-six Europeans, from 300 to 400 drilled native troops, and six guns. However, he prepared for a vigorous defence. But the odds were too great. On the 6th of September, after a resistance which had lasted twelve days, he was forced to demand a parley. The parley resulted two days later in a capitulation, the terms of which stipulated that Martin and his co-patriots should be shipped to Europe either that year or the beginning of the next. Meanwhile, they were allowed to march out with all the honours of war. The native troops were simply disbanded.

Severe and apparently fatal as was this blow, it resulted favourably to the young settlement. Martin and his companions were despatched to France. The reception accorded to Martin there, alike by the King and the Directors, was cordial in the extreme. The latter then, apparently for the first time, appreciated the greatness of their agent's character. And when, four years after the capture (September 21, 1697), the peace of Ryswick restored Pondichery to France, Martin was re-appointed Governor, and was despatched thither with 200 regular troops, several engineers, a large supply of military stores, several heavy and field guns, and materials in abundance for the use of the settlement.

Martin was now not only Governor of Pondichery; by letters patent from the King, he was nominated, February, 1701, Director-General of all the French possessions in India. Those possessions included a small plot of ground, about six acres, at Masulipatám, called the French Pata, acquired by Mercara; of a decaying establishment of about eight acres at Surat, abandoned in 1714; of the settlement of Chandarnagar on the right bank of the Húglí, twenty-two miles from Calcutta, first occupied by a small body of Frenchmen in 1676, and regularly ceded to them by the Emperor Aurangzib in 1688; and of six small plots of ground, comprising a total of about forty-six acres, at Calicut, Balasor, Dacca, Patná, Kásimbázár, and Jogdiá.

It was unfortunate that the failures at Madagascar had dealt so hardly with the fortunes of the Company that the Directors were unable to extend to Martin the full support necessary for the profitable development of the affairs of the French settlements in India. But Martin conquered the impossible, and when he died on the 30th December, 1706, there were grouped round the rising and prosperous town which gave its name to the colony 40,000 natives, whose prosperity depended upon the trade with France. French influence, moreover, was all-powerful with the native chiefs and princes in the vicinity. Martin had made it a cardinal point of his policy to attach those chiefs and princes to the French settlement by appealing alike to their interest and their self-love, two matters with regard to which they were peculiarly sensitive. His success, therefore, far from evoking envy or apprehension, produced only satisfaction and contentment. French good offices were constantly employed to settle local disputes, and when he died, the evidences of the esteem in which he had been held were overwhelming.

Eight years after the death of Martin, the fifty years' monopoly granted by Louis XIV to the Company in 1664 expired. It had long been in a moribund condition. Two years before the expiration of its Charter, its resources had been reduced to so low an ebb that it had been forced from want of means to transfer to some merchants of St. Malo its rights of trading to the East in consideration of an annual payment. This destitution produced its natural effects in India. Debts which had been contracted at Surat remained unpaid, and although MM. Dulivier and Hébert, the immediate successors of Martin, continued to administer the affairs of the settlement at Pondichery on the principles he had established, the falling off in the carrying-trade reduced them to very great straits. Nor, after lingering painfully for ten years, did there appear any reasonable chance of amendment. Indeed, just before the expiry of its Charter the friends of the Company had interest sufficient to procure the extension for ten years of its powers. This meant ten years more of atrophy. But in September of the year from which the continuation of the Charter dated (1715), Louis XIV died. The Regency of the Duke of Orleans succeeded, and within a month of his accession to that high office, there appeared in Paris a young Scotchman whose soaring genius captivated for a few years the hearts of all classes, and whose schemes promised to impart new vitality to the world of commerce.

France then possessed other territories beyond Europe, besides her small settlements in India. In 1525 she had acquired Canada; in 1682 she had explored and taken possession of Louisiana; in August,

1717, Law formed and presented to the public a Company, called the Company of the West, with a capital of 100,000,000 francs, to possess for twenty-four years the entire monopoly of the trade with Canada and Louisiana. He allowed this scheme to dangle before the public for nearly two years, whilst engaged in those speculations nearer home with which his name is so fatally connected. In May, 1719, however, he took in hand the scheme of the Company of the West, and persuading the Regent to suppress by an edict the privileges of the moribund Companies of India and of China, he transferred all their privileges, all their possessions, all their liabilities,—in a word, the remnant of all that they had acquired, and all that they owed,—to the Company of the West. By the eleventh article of the edict, it was directed that the Company should thenceforth be styled the 'Company of the Indies,' and should assume the arms of the Company of the West.

For a brief period it seemed as though the new Company would achieve a brilliant success. Its shares speedily rose to a premium of 200 per cent. It purchased from the Government for 4,020,000 francs the monopoly of tobacco, a purchase which was so profitable that it enabled them to return an annual revenue of 8,000,000 francs, equivalent to eight per cent. of the total capital of the Company as it was fixed in 1725. But at last, and within a brief period, the crash came. In the summer of 1720 a panic set in. The shares fell to the lowest depths. Everything foreboded a catastrophe. In the height of the crisis, the Directors of the Company of the Indies stepped forward with the offer to take up all the depreciated notes of the Royal Bank, and to extinguish them at the rate of 50,000,000 francs a month for one year, provided its privileges were made perpetual. The Government accepted the offer, and issued a decree declaring the privileges accorded to the Company of the Indies to be perpetual. Thenceforth the Company assumed the title of 'Perpetual Company of the Indies.'

But the change in its condition was not confined to the grant of perpetuity of privileges. In October of the same year the Government made a return to cash payments; dissolved the connection between the Company and the Royal Bank; and enabled the former to reorganise itself on the footing of a commercial association independent of the State. On the retreat of Law, shortly afterwards, an inquiry took place—under the supervision of a Board appointed by the Government—into the affairs of the Company. The result of the investigations, cancellings, and changes effected by this Board was to leave the Company (1723) a private commercial association, with a capital of 112,000,000 francs in 56,000 shares. Two years later the capital was reduced, by the cancellation of 5,000 shares, to 102,000,000. At this figure it remained. But of all the great privileges conceded to it by Law, such as the coining of money, the collection of the revenues of the State, and others, there remained only the monopoly of tobacco and the grant of perpetuity. In other respects it was placed upon the footing of the original Company founded by Colbert in 1664.

Meanwhile the agents of the Company at Pondichery were exerting themselves to maintain, with insufficient means, the position acquired for the settlement by Martin. In 1718 M. de la Provostière had succeeded Hébert. On his death in 1721 M. Lenoir, a man of ability and energy, assumed the reins of office. Then it was that affairs took a turn for the better. The Company formed by Law had taken the earliest opportunity to despatch to India three merchantmen, richly laden, and these arrived just as Lenoir assumed office. Their coming was most opportune. The credit of the settlement was at its lowest ebb. Debts contracted at Surat, and at the other small factories previously mentioned, were crying loud against the Company. In the profits to be made from the cargoes of the new arrivals Lenoir, a prudent man, recognised the means of restoring the Company's credit. He used them for that purpose. The remedy, though great for the moment, was but transitory in its effects. The financial crash, and its consequence to the fortunes of the Company in Paris, reacted in India. For the three years that followed no ships arrived from Europe. In 1723 the settlement was reduced to the direst straits. The local agents had neither money, nor merchandise, nor resources. Lenoir, too, on the strength of the promise made him on his assumption of office, that he should receive yearly shipments of goods, had entered into contracts with the native merchants for the supply of return cargoes. But for the confidence which had been nurtured by Martin, and maintained by his successors, the outlook would have been ruinous indeed. As it was, the native merchants, recognising that the fault did not lie with Lenoir, agreed to wait for better times.

The process of reconstitution through which the Company passed in 1723 gave it renewed life. At the end of that year two ships arrived, and from that time to 1726 three or four ships came every year. From 1726 the progress was more rapid still. The results to the settlement were most beneficial. Some idea of it may be realised from the fact that in September 1729, and in January 1730, Lenoir was able to transmit to France merchandise to the value of 5,500,000 francs, a large amount in those days for a young settlement. With returning prosperity, came the embellishment of the town. Tasteful houses were erected, a college was built, gardens were laid out, a stately edifice for the accommodation of foreign envoys rose in its turn from the ground. At the same time, the convictions of the natives were respected, for whilst other houses were cleared away, the pagodas and temples of the Hindus remained unmolested.

The prosperity continued unbroken during the remaining years of the administration of Lenoir. But, in 1735, that able man was succeeded by a Governor in no respect his inferior, probably, indeed, even more qualified than he was to deal with the state of civil war then about to supervene throughout the length and breadth of the Karnátik. This was M. Benoit Dumas.

M. Dumas had entered the service of the Company founded by Colbert shortly before its extinction, in 1713. He was then seventeen. At Pondichery, whither he proceeded immediately, he gave proofs of rare capacity, and, after a stay there of nearly eight years, he was transferred to the Isle of France and Bourbon to administer affairs in those islands. He held that office till 1735, when he was nominated to succeed Lenoir at Pondichery. His character was that of a prudent man, a lover of peace, but resolute, jealous of the honour and interests of France, yet willing to act only when circumstances should indicate that such action would be beneficial.

Dumas had not been many months in India before circumstances arose which required the decision of a man of action. The Nuwábs of the Karnátik had, since the invasion of Sívájí, previously referred to, cultivated friendship with the rulers of Pondichery. The actual Nuwáb, at the time of the arrival of M. Dumas, Dost Alí by name, had displayed more than an ordinary desire to cultivate intimate relations with the new Governor. Dumas had not been many months at his post before it occurred to him that he might utilise this friendship to obtain some permanent advantage for the Company. In return, then, for some slight services, he asked the Nuwáb to obtain from the Court of Delhi permission to coin money. This request was granted, to the great monetary advantage and increase of prestige of the French. Two years later (1738), Dumas was tempted by an offer from the pretender to the throne of Tanjore to cede to him certain districts if the French Governor would lend him material aid for the recovery of his territories. It was indeed a tempting offer, for the districts offered were those which would give the French a hold on the sea-coast of Tanjore. To accede to it, however, would be to depart from the principle of strict neutrality in the quarrels of native princes hitherto pursued. But the risk, in the opinion of Dumas, was greatly outweighed by the advantages. He accepted then the offer; supplied the pretender with money, with gunpowder, and with warlike stores; and received in return a grant of the town of Kárikál, of the adjoining fort of Karkan-Garhí, and of ten villages depending upon them. The actual cession was dated February 14, 1739.

The possession of this territory gave the French a footing in the kingdom of Tanjore, which enabled them to overshadow the influence of the Dutch, whose factory was at Nágápatnam, a few miles lower down the coast. The acquisition increased the power, the manner in which it had been acquired increased the influence, of the Pondichery settlement. But, the year following, it seemed as though the fortunes of the settlement would be imperilled. At the close of 1739 the Maráthás, jealous of Muhammadan preponderance in Southern India, invaded the Karnátik; surprised (May 19, 1740) the army of Dost Alí at the Damálcherí Pass; and completely defeated it. Dost Alí, his second son, and almost all his chief officers, were left dead on the field. The catastrophe, overwhelming in many respects as it seemed, served to illustrate the regard and confidence with which the foreigners at Pondichery had inspired the chiefs and landowners of the Karnátik. With an unanimity which was not the result of concert, these turned at once to Pondichery for protection. No other place on the coast or in the interior offered to their interested eyes so certain a protection. For days and days after the defeat had become known the natives of the surrounding districts poured into Pondichery, bringing with them their families and their valuables. Five days after the battle the widow of the slain Nuwáb, her children, her dependents, and an escort guarding her jewels and other property, were received in state by M. Dumas. That prudent man knew well that such an act might bring upon him the wrath and the armies of the Maráthás. But, he argued, boldness is often prudence. For some days preceding, and for many days to follow, stores of grain had entered and did enter the town. In the face of a great crisis Dumas had deliberately chosen the line, which, if attended with great risk, promised him, should the risk be successfully encountered, the greatest advantage. In the same spirit he granted the hospitality of Pondichery to the wife and daughter of Chanda Sáhíb, the son-in-law of the late Nuwáb. He was glad that in the hour of imminent peril it should fall to the lot of France to afford protection to those who unquestionably would, on the retirement of the Maráthás, recover supreme power in the Karnátik.

He had reasoned justly. It is true that the Maráthá leader, incensed by the reception granted to the relatives of the late Nuwáb, and by the refusal of the French Governor to surrender them to his mercy, threatened to deal to Pondichery the fate of Bassein, then recently captured from the Portuguese; that he detached a body of 16,000 troops to convert his threats into deeds; that these troops captured and pillaged Porto Novo, thirty-two miles to the south of Pondichery, and Gudalar, belonging to the English, sixteen miles nearer to it; that they reached a point within five miles of Pondichery itself. Thence their leader despatched an envoy to demand, on the penalty of dealing with it as he had dealt with Trichinopoly, then recently taken, the surrender of the town. Dumas, equal to the occasion, hid nothing from the envoy. He showed him his supplies, his fortifications, his guns, his drilled Europeans, his drilled sipáhis, and then told him that, so equipped, Pondichery would resist to the last. To show his friendly disposition, however, he gave to the envoy, as he departed, a present of ten bottles of Nantes cordials, to be delivered to his chief. It would seem that the wife of the chief tasted these cordials, and insisted upon obtaining more. The storming of Pondichery being recognised as difficult, the chief determined to proceed by way of negotiation. The result was that Dumas made him a present of thirty bottles in addition, and he, withdrawing all his demands, returned to Western India.

In the interval Pondichery had received other visitors, among them Safdar Alí, son and successor of the late Nuwáb. This chief was so impressed by the conduct of M. Dumas, that on the departure of the Maráthás he increased the French territory by the cession of land bringing a yearly revenue of 10,000 rupees. The Subahdár of the Deccan, the representative of the Mughal in Southern India, marked his appreciation of the conduct of M. Dumas by transmitting to him a letter of thanks and a dress of honour. Safdar Alí, besides the territory referred to, sent him the armour of his deceased father, richly adorned with gold and precious stones, together with three elephants, several horses, many swords and jewelled weapons, and a letter of honour. The King of Delhi himself, Muhammad Sháh, conferred upon him the title of Nuwáb; the rank of Commander of 4,500 horse, 2,000 of whom he was to be allowed to keep about his person in times of peace, without being at charge for their maintenance. Dumas, always eager for the interests of France, and conscious how much the natives were impressed by the possession of such dignities, asked, and obtained sanction, that these honours might be regarded as transferable to his successor.

Before the crisis, the result of which I have just related, had occurred, Dumas had transmitted to France his request that he might be relieved at the first convenient opportunity. Towards its conclusion he received an intimation that the Court of Directors had accepted his resignation, and had nominated as his successor, M. Joseph Francis Dupleix, then Intendant of Chandarnagar. The new Governor arrived at Pondichery in October, 1741, took the oaths of Director-General of the French possessions in India, and declared himself to be the Nuwáb of the Mughal, and a Commander of 4,500 Horse.

The records of the six years' administration of M. Dumas prove that he was no unworthy successor to Francis Martin. He had displayed to a very high degree boldness, tact, prudence, and skill. He had greatly increased the prestige of the French, and had added considerably to their possessions. On the other hand, it has to be recollected that he accomplished these results by departing from the line of strict neutrality which Martin had laid down. He had the choice either to do that or to succumb. Probably, under the circumstances, Martin would have acted similarly. His prudent boldness had given the settlement a position which, in the crash of a decaying empire, might be improved to a degree till then undreamt of. Everything depended on the character of his successor. Dumas had clearly indicated the direction. He had secured recognition of French influence and French prestige. We have now to note the manner in which Dupleix turned to still greater account the opportunities which arose from the action of his capable predecessor.

CHAPTER II

THE SYSTEM OF DUPLEIX

JOSEPH FRANCIS DUPLEIX was born at Landrecies in 1697. From an early age he was destined by his father, who was Farmer-General and Director-General of the Company of the Indies[1], to a commercial career. To such a career the boy, who had displayed a strong inclination for the exact sciences, shewed a decided aversion. To cure him, his father sent him, at the age of seventeen, to sea. The result corresponded to his hopes. The young sailor returned from his voyages on the Atlantic and Indian oceans anxious to take a part in the world of enterprise and commerce, ready to bend himself to his father's will. The father responded by obtaining for him a high post in the service of the Company of the Indies at Pondichery. Dupleix joined his appointment in 1720. He soon came to the conclusion that it would be possible to make Pondichery the principal emporium of trade in southern India. The Governor, Lenoir, whilst recognising the feasibility of the plan, was deterred from

[1] His full titles were: 'Écuyer, seigneur de Bacquencourt et de Mercin, seigneur des gardes Fauneville, La Bruyère, etc., écuyer ordinaire de la grande écurie de sa Majesté, Fermier Général et Directeur Général de la Compagnie des Indes.'

prosecuting it with vigour by the poverty of the settlement. Dupleix then gave in his own person a practical proof how his plan, conducted on a system, must lead to fortune. He embarked in private trade with the interior—a practice then sanctioned by the regulations of the Company—and in a short time succeeded in amassing a considerable fortune.

The changes in the constitution of the parent Company at home, duly noted in the preceding chapter, had caused frictions and misunderstandings in the settlement. As a consequence of one of these Dupleix was (December, 1726) suspended from his office by the orders of the Directors, and offered a free passage to France. Dupleix declined to avail himself of the offer, but remained at Pondichery whilst he appealed against the unjust order. At the end of four years the falseness of the charges preferred against him was recognised (September 30, 1730), and the Directors, to compensate him for the injustice he had suffered, nominated him, shortly afterwards, Intendant of Chandarnagar. Thither, accordingly, Dupleix proceeded.

How Chandarnagar had been occupied in 1676, and regularly ceded by the Mughal Emperor in 1688, has been stated in a previous page. Since that period the history of the little settlement had not been a history of success. It had suffered, more even than Pondichery, from the poverty of the Company. Stagnation had become the rule there. The Company's agents, with no means, and little energy, had drifted into a life of sloth and lassitude. Their utmost endeavours were directed to surmount pressing emergencies. The place bore evidence of the want of enterprise of its occupants. It had a ruined and forlorn appearance. Its silent walls were overgrown with jungle. And whilst the swift stream of the Huglí carried past it merchandise from the interior intended for the rivals who were converting the mud huts of Chatánatí into the substantial warehouses of old Calcutta, the landing-places of Chandarnagar were comparatively deserted.

Such was Chandarnagar when Dupleix arrived there as Intendant in 1731. Decaying and lifeless though he found the place, he regarded its position with other feelings than those of anxiety and dismay. He saw that it had capabilities; that it might be made as prosperous as Chatánatí; that energy and prudence, directing capital, could accomplish results which would startle his sluggish colleagues. He set to work with a will; employed the fortune he had accumulated at Pondichery in the purchase of ships; freighted cargoes; opened communications with the interior; induced native merchants to settle in the town. His compatriots, gained by his energy, joined him in the race for prosperity. He had room for all. To some he advanced money, others he took into partnership, all he encouraged. Chandarnagar soon felt the effect of the master's hand. Four years after his arrival the settlement which, in 1731, had but half a dozen country-boats lying unemployed at the landing-place, could boast of some thirty or forty vessels, small and large, at sea, engaged in conveying the products of Bengal to Jeddo, to Mocha, to Basrah, to Surat, and to China. Before he left, the number had increased to seventy. To produce such results, Dupleix had opened communications with the chief places in the interior, even with Thibet. The resurrection of the settlement gave the greatest satisfaction in France, and it was the character of the man who had made possible such a revival, prosperous alike to the settlers and their masters, that prompted the Perpetual Company of the Indies to nominate its Intendant successor to M. Dumas at Pondichery.

Before Dupleix left Chandarnagar he married, April 17, 1741, a lady of great ability, and whose advice he always prized above the advice of others. This lady was a widow, the daughter of M. Albert, a surgeon of the Company at Pondichery. She had married M. Vincens, a member of the superior Council at that town, in 1719, and had borne him six children. M. Vincens died at Chandarnagar in 1739 or 1740, and Dupleix married the widow, as above stated, in April, 1741. I have before me a copy of the 'act of marriage.' It shows that the ceremony was performed with considerable ceremonial; that Dupleix, aged forty-three, was at the time President of the superior Council of Pondichery, and General Commandant of the French possessions in India; that his wife was thirty-three. Of Madame Dupleix I find it recorded that her wise counsels and her energy sustained her husband in all his trials. She was with him during the whole period of his administration of French India. And when that administration came to a close, in the manner to be related, she accompanied him to France, to die there of the chagrin caused by the injustice meted out to the husband she adored.

Dupleix found the lands of the French settlement on the southern coast suffering from the effects of the Maráthá invasion. Those marauding warriors had, after the manner of locusts, eaten up the products, and by their presence prevented the tilling of the soil for the coming season. The Karnátik, too, unsettled by the fatal invasion, was threatened by the Subahdár of the Deccan. There were indications, moreover, that in Europe a war between France and England was imminent, and it was necessary to foresee and to provide for the necessities which such an event might entail on the Indian settlements.

To be able to meet difficulties from without, it was necessary, in the opinion of Dupleix, to be prepared at home. He therefore proceeded to put his house in order. He set on foot inquiries having for their object the checking of public expenditure, increasing, as he thought, unnecessarily. He issued regulations to put a stop to the habit of taking douceurs, a habit borrowed from the natives. He thoroughly overhauled the fortifications. He notified at the same time to the native princes in the Karnátik and at Haidarábád his succession to M. Dumas alike as Director-General of the French settlements and as recipient of the honours conferred upon the holder of that office by the King of Delhi, whilst from those of inferior rank in the neighbourhood he received personal homage. Having seen these matters in progress he proceeded to Chandarnagar, to be installed there as Nuwáb. When this ceremony, conducted with the pomp so dear to the people of India, had been concluded, he expressed a desire to pay a visit to the Muhammadan Commandant of the town of Húglí. The latter, however, recognising the superior rank of the Frenchman, insisted with that courtesy innate in the truest type of Islám on paying the first visit. The honours with which Dupleix was received made a deep impression on the natives. On his return, after the ceremony, to Pondichery, he acted there on the same principle. Knowing that the princelets about him recognised display as a symbol of power, he acted so that they should see in him an officer holding his honours direct from the Court of Delhi. To strengthen this feeling he left nothing undone in the way of magnificence of surroundings. Troublous times were coming. In the event of an attack made by a European power, much, he felt, would depend upon the position the French settlement occupied in native opinion. He strove then to act towards the natives, princes as well as people, in the manner which his experience had proved was that best calculated to gain their esteem.

Had Dupleix at this crisis been supported largely and liberally from France he might have established the settlement on a basis which would have made it the first of the European settlements in southern India. But at the very moment when he should have received support, he met only with discouragement. In a despatch dated September 18, 1743, the Directors of the Perpetual Company informed him that in view of the probability of a war between France and England they were compelled to restrict the number of their vessels for India to four, two of which only were destined for Pondichery. They pressed upon him at the same time the necessity of reducing his expenses by at least one-half; and of suspending all outlay on account of the fortifications.

How to act in the face of such an order? Such was the question Dupleix had to solve. The order regarding the fortifications touched him most. He knew, and he was aware that the Directors knew, that the defences of Pondichery were in a state almost to invite attack. The original fortifications were crumbling, and, on the side of the sea—the side which specially required protection—there was a space of a thousand toises absolutely open. The way in which Dupleix acted on this occasion affords a key to his character. Recognising that, under the circumstances, to obey was to invite destruction, and that, as Director-General, he was really though not nominally responsible to the France which he represented, he disobeyed the order. Along the entire front of the space spoken of he erected a solid rampart with a broad ditch in front and rear. He had amassed by successful trading a considerable fortune. A portion of this he devoted without stint to the work. From the same source he provided cargoes for the two vessels which, in pursuance of the advices he had received, arrived from France that year, and which, but for his liberality and enterprise, would have returned empty. The other order of the Company he carried out with rigour. He reduced salaries, removed abuses, strangled corruption, until, in spite of the murmurs of some and the more open complaints of others, he brought about the required balance between income and expenditure. The Directors warmly approved all that he had done. His conduct in furnishing cargoes to their vessels caused them to overlook his disobedience regarding the fortifications. Regarding the former they wrote him that they had been 'much pleased at the zeal which he and the Councils of Pondichery and Chandarnagar have displayed for our interests in procuring cargoes for our two ships.' With respect to the fortifications, which took more than two years to complete, they wrote to him under date November 30, 1746: 'The promptitude with which the town of Pondichery has been enclosed on the side facing the sea has given us real pleasure. We are under a great obligation to you on that account:' further, 'we have seen with not the less satisfaction all the measures you have taken, both to provide, notwithstanding your poverty, cargoes for the ships, the sailing of which we had announced to you.'

In 1744 the war of the Austrian succession broke

out in Europe. France and England were ranged on opposite sides. For the first time since the French had settled at Pondichery the two nations were at war. The English had occupied a small point on the eastern coast, eighty-six miles above Pondichery, in 1639, and had built on that plot a fort which they had called Fort St. George. The natives called the plot Chennapatanam, the English gave it the name Madras. The locality had not been carefully selected. The roadstead, from October to January, was dangerous. The soil of the country about the fort was dry and sterile, and the country itself was but scantily populated. Nevertheless, the enterprise of the English had overcome some of these obstacles and had defied others. A considerable native population had gathered round the place, and the vessels which came every year from Europe succeeded in landing and taking their cargoes without much damage. At the moment when France declared war against England (March, 1744) the chief of the English settlement was Governor Morse, a merchant engaged all his life in trade, and not very conversant with politics.

Although France had declared war against England, the English Government had taken a far wider grasp of the situation which such a declaration might produce than had the Government of France. The story of the prosperity of Pondichery and the versatile talent of its Governor had reached England, and, on the declaration of war, the English Ministry despatched orders to Commodore Barnett, then on the Eastern station, to proceed to the eastern coast of India, and employ there his superiority of force to the best advantage. The preparations of the French Government were not nearly so forward. The Directors of the Perpetual Company wrote, however, to Dupleix to inform him that they had instructed M. de la Bourdonnais, Governor of the Isles of France and Bourbon, to sail with a squadron to his assistance. Meanwhile they urged him to endeavour to come to an understanding with Governor Morse, to plead that the settlements had no cause of quarrel, and to suggest that they should remain neutral during the war of their principals.

Dupleix did not consider the proposition as either practical or possible. He made it nevertheless. But Morse saw only the immediate advantage. The British squadron might arrive at any moment. Then Pondichery would be at his mercy. He did not care to imagine that possibly the day might arrive when the situations would be inverted. He pleaded therefore the orders he had received from England, and declined the proposal.

Almost simultaneously with the receipt of this reply came information from the islands that La Bourdonnais had sent back his squadron to France. Left then to his own resources, Dupleix set to work to find a method of baffling the greed of his rivals, and he found it. Pondichery itself was powerless, for the rampart he was building was not nearly completed, and he could dispose of but 436 Europeans. But at this crisis the friendly relations he had been careful to cultivate with the native princes bore a rich and abundant fruit. Dupleix wrote to the Nuwáb of the Karnátik, reminded him of the friendly relations which had existed between the French settlement and his predecessors; of the moral support rendered by Pondichery to the Karnátik ruler at the time of the Maráthá invasion; of the desire of the French to live at peace with all around them; and begged him to employ his authority to prevent his tenants, the English, from attacking a settlement, the chief of which was an officer of the Great Mughal, and his own friend.

The Nuwáb, Anwáru' dín, had but recently succeeded to his office, but he was cognisant of all the circumstances referred to by Dupleix. Neither he, nor any man in India, regarded the scattered European settlers on isolated parts of the coast as possessing claims to be seriously reckoned with. They were vassals of the lord paramount, simple traders dependent upon his goodwill, nothing more. But the French had the character of being polite, friendly, unaggressive, desirous to conciliate. They had had, too, opportunities of displaying their sympathy. The manner in which they had used those opportunities had made an impression. Anwáru' dín then acted in the spirit of the request preferred to him by Dupleix. He informed Morse that he would not permit him to attack the French settlement. He added that in similar circumstances he would forbid the French to attack the English settlement.

For the moment, then, Dupleix was safe. But the English squadron had arrived, and on the side of the sea Pondichery was virtually blockaded. There was still then cause for anxiety. The reader can imagine, then, the reaction of joy which was produced by the arrival of information from a sure source (May, 1746) that the long-despaired-of squadron of La Bourdonnais had been sighted off the western coast.

La Bourdonnais, after an early career full of promise, had succeeded, in 1735, M. Dumas as Governor of the Isles of France and Bourbon. It is not too much to say that by his own teaching and example he had laid the foundation of the future prosperity of those islands. He had proceeded to France in 1740 with the object of personally convincing the French Government of the enormous advantage which must accrue to the French possessions in India, if, in the event of a war with England, they had a certain base of operations in the Indian Ocean, where land-forces could be trained, and whence ships could sally to prey upon the commerce of their rivals; that they actually possessed in the two islands such a base, and it was only necessary that he should have the ships and the men. After many rebuffs La Bourdonnais succeeded in convincing Cardinal Fleury of the reasonableness of his contention, and in 1741 he proceeded to the islands with five ships belonging to the Company. Hardly had he arrived there when information reached him of the dangers threatening Pondichery from the invasion of the Maráthás, referred to in a previous page. He sailed then for that place, found that the tact of M. Dumas had averted the danger, but that Mahé, on the western coast, was threatened. Thither then he proceeded, and having ensured its safety, returned to the islands. On his arrival there he was met by an order from Cardinal Fleury to send back his ships to France, that pacific statesman fearing lest the English should take umbrage at the presence of such an armament off the coasts of India. La Bourdonnais obeyed, sent back his ships, and tendered his resignation. Meanwhile Fleury had died. A few months later war was declared. The position which La Bourdonnais had foreseen, and to meet which he had made his journey to France, had arrived, but the folly of his superiors had torn from his hands the weapon with which he would have conjured the storm. Sensible too late of their folly, the Government ordered him to remain at his post and do his best. Brave and resolute, La Bourdonnais threw his soul into the task; improvised a fleet, trained sailors, drilled soldiers, laid hands on all the vessels which came from France, and on June 1, 1746, sailed with nine ships, poorly armed and badly manned, to carry aid to the threatened settlements of France in southern India. Towards the end of the month he was off Mahé, learnt there that the English squadron had been last heard of off Nágápatnam, near the French settlement of Kárikál, and that it was waiting there to intercept him. He sailed at once to meet it, encountered it, commanded by Commodore Peyton, off Nágápatnam, fought with it an action, indecisive indeed, but the result of which was to cause Peyton to abandon the eastern coast to his enemy and to sail for Trinkámalí; and anchored two days later in the roadstead of Pondichery.

Then there came into contact two men, both clothed with authority, each of whom desired to be first, and neither of whom would be content with the rôle of second. Up to the day of meeting each had professed the most earnest desire to co-operate with the other. 'The honour of success,' Dupleix had written in the early part of the year, 'will be yours, and I shall hold myself fortunate in contributing thereto through means which owe their value entirely to your skill.' On his side La Bourdonnais had written: 'We ought to regard one another as equally interested in the progress of events, and work in concert. For my part, Sir, I devote myself to you beforehand, and I swear to you a perfect confidence.' Such had been their professions before they had met, when danger seemed very close to the French settlement. But they had not met an hour before the question arose which of the two men, the one Director-General of all the French possessions in India, the other Admiral of the fleet which he had formed, and manned, and instructed himself, was to be supreme. The English fleet had disappeared. Madras was open to attack. If only it were possible to obtain the tacit consent of the Nuwáb the French could visit the English settlement with the fate with which her Governor and the Commodore acting in concert with him had threatened Pondichery. The question seemed to depend upon a cordial understanding between the French Governor and the French Admiral. Madras was comparatively defenceless. The best chance for her safety lay in the possibility of a disagreement, or want of cordial action, between Dupleix and La Bourdonnais.

CHAPTER III

The First Blow for Predominance

Into the details of the quarrel between the chief civil authority in India and the commander of the fleet, I shall enter only so far as they affect the main object of my book. By the orders transmitted to him from Paris, La Bourdonnais was compelled to admit the superior authority on land of the Director-General of the French settlements in India. The idea of the capture of Madras had been a leading idea alike with Dupleix and La Bourdonnais. Yet, now that the hour had arrived to strike the blow, whilst Dupleix remained firm and constant to his purpose, La Bourdonnais shewed a disposition to hold back. He proposed first to attack Fort St. David, a fort purchased in 1691 by the English, near the town of Gudálur, sixteen miles south of Pondichery, and which at one time had been their head-quarters. When Dupleix protested against this proceeding as too petty, La Bourdonnais declared he would sail in pursuit of the English fleet. He did sail, caught sight of it, but unable to bring it to action, returned, the 25th of August, to Pondichery. There again he displayed great unwillingness to undertake the expedition against Madras. The burden of his objection was that it would be dangerous to attack Madras until the English fleet should have been destroyed. He dwelt, moreover, on the perils to which he would expose his ships by remaining on the coast after the 15th of October, about which date the monsoon was accustomed to come on with a fury dangerous to ships anchored in an open roadstead, exposed to its full force. At last, the 27th of August, Dupleix unable to persuade, acting in concert with his Council, served on the admiral a summons, calling upon him 'on the part of the King and the Company to make choice of one of the two plans' they had presented to him the day previous. The first of these plans prescribed an attack on Madras, the second, the pursuit and destruction of the English fleet. They added: 'these are the only plans we consider practicable, suitable to present circumstances, to the glory of the King, to the honour of the Nation, to the interests of the Company, to the strength of his squadron, and the weakness of his enemies by sea and land.' These plans were plainly specified. La Bourdonnais was required either to attack Madras, or to sail in pursuit of the English fleet.

In consequence of this citation La Bourdonnais sailed for Madras the evening of the 12th of September, joined his fleet—which he had despatched on the 28th of August with orders to anchor off the Madras coast—on the 14th, landed 600 men with two guns the same evening twelve miles south of the English fort, and increasing them on the 15th to 1100 Europeans, 400 sipáhis, and about the same number of Africans brought from the Islands, he marched on Fort St. George, and summoned it to surrender.

Governor Morse was in no condition to offer a resistance likely to prove successful. At the moment Fort St. George contained behind its ramparts only some 300 soldiers, but of these only 200 were fit for duty. It is true that amongst its merchants or factors there was the budding genius destined, a few years later, to baffle all the plans of Dupleix, but whose brilliant talents were concealed at the time behind a morose exterior and by intense depression of spirits. But the situation was too desperate to be affected even by the genius which Robert Clive was soon to develope. Governor Morse, indeed, attempted to obtain from the Nuwáb of the Karnátik the same protection which that ruler had accorded to Pondichery. But he approached him unskilfully, and his messenger was dismissed without an answer. He could do no more. On the 21st, then, he surrendered the fort and its dependencies to La Bourdonnais, the garrison becoming prisoners of war.

Into the contention which followed between La Bourdonnais and Dupleix as to whether the right to dispose of the conquered place rested with the Commander of the fleet or with the Governor and Council of Pondichery, it is foreign to the purpose of this work to enter. It must suffice to state that the Home Government decided in a despatch sent in anticipation, it would seem, of a conflict of authority in favour of

Dupleix, and, after a delay of nearly five weeks, characterised by the most unseemly contentions between the representatives of the Civil and Naval power of France on the coast, La Bourdonnais handed over Fort St. George and its dependencies to M. Desprémesnil, a member of the Pondichery Council, on the 23rd of October, and having as far as possible repaired the damages done to his fleet by the bursting of the monsoon on the 15th, sailed, first for Pondichery, and ultimately to the islands, and thence to France.

Sole master now of the situation in India, Dupleix, whose clear brain as yet only aspired to make France supreme, if not alone, amongst the European nations on the coast, set himself to gain, if it were possible, the assent of the Nuwáb of the Karnátik to the retention by France of her conquest. He had induced the Nuwáb to assent to his attack upon Madras by an assurance that, the place once taken, he would transfer it to the Nuwáb himself. Possibly, at the time he made this promise, he was sincere. But the long delay caused by the refusal of La Bourdonnais to transfer the fort to the Pondichery authorities had changed the position. The Nuwáb, mistrusting the assurances of Dupleix, that the delay in making over Fort St. George to his agents was caused by the insubordinate action of the French officer in command, had displayed all the angry feelings of an irresponsible ruler who feels that he has been duped, and, even before La Bourdonnais had departed, he had begun to collect troops in the vicinity of the fort to compel its transfer. Dupleix was neither blind nor indifferent to the coming danger. But his position was bristling with difficulties. La Bourdonnais had entered into a compact with the English for the ultimate restoration to them of Fort St. George. Dupleix had, at the time, absolutely refused to recognise the compact. The French force had been able, he argued, to compel the surrender of Madras without conditions. He would then ratify no arrangement of that character, made contrary to his express directions, and therefore *ultra vires.* His position with respect to the Nuwáb was altogether different. To obtain his permission to attack Madras he had promised to transfer it to that prince. But, now that he had it, he was determined to use all the means at his disposal to endeavour to creep out of this obligation. His heart had already begun to swell with hopes of expelling the English traders from all their possessions on the coast, and he feared lest the Nuwáb might restore to them the conquest which he had been at such pains to make for France. Had a good understanding with La Bourdonnais been possible he might have indulged in a still more soaring vision. Had that admiral, before the monsoon broke, sailed for the Húglí with his fleet he might have effected at Chatánatí (Calcutta) that which he had accomplished at Madras, and given his countrymen not merely supremacy, but undivided sway from the Húglí to Cape Comorin.

But La Bourdonnais had gone. One part of the dream could however be accomplished if he could retain Madras. To effect this end Dupleix exhausted all his powers of diplomacy. But the Nuwáb was thoroughly roused. He and his advisers felt that they had been duped, and they did not like it. The Nuwáb continued then his preparations, and sent his son, Máphúz Khán, to lead against Fort St. George the levies he had raised. Dupleix, resolved to retain it, sent instructions to Desprémesnil to defend Fort St. George at all hazards, promising him a speedy re-inforcement. Máphúz Khán, at the head of 10,000 men, mostly cavalry, had appeared before Madras about the 25th of October, and a few days later reduced the garrison of about 500 men to great extremities by cutting off their water supply. To recover the springs Desprémesnil ordered, on the 2nd of November, a sally of 400 men accompanied by two field-pieces. It was the first contest between the European settlers and the soldiers of the soil, and it was a type of all that were to follow. The two guns did the business. The natives had been accustomed to long intervals between each discharge. They were not disconcerted then by the opening fire. But the almost immediate discharge of the same guns surprised, the third frightened them, and they fled in dismay. They had lost 70 men, the French had not a single man wounded.

But in a few hours the panic in the Nuwáb's camp subsided, and when scouts informed Máphúz Khán that a relieving French force, consisting of but 230 Europeans and 700 sipáhis, without a single gun, was approaching, he fearlessly led a force of 10,000 men to dispute with them the passage of the river Adyár. The relieving force was commanded by an Engineer officer of great ability, named Paradis. He reached the northern bank of the Adyár on the 4th of November, only to see on the opposite bank the serried ranks of the enemy. There was no turning the position. He must dare to trust the interests of his countrymen in a very unequal contest, or to retreat. Not for a second did he hesitate. Fording the river, he directed one volley at the masses in front of him, and charged. The effect was electric. The native troops, unaccustomed to such prompt audacity, fled, panic-stricken. An opportune sally from Fort St. George completed their discomfiture. Never was a victory more complete or more decisive.

It was, indeed, a battle to be remembered. The success of the first sortie from Madras had been attributed by the natives to the novel method of the artillery fire. But, on the Adyár, the French had not a single gun: Máphúz Khán had many. The battle was won by boldness, by élan, by dash, by daring to affront danger. It was this battle, called after the place near which it was fought, the battle of St. Thomé, which inverted the position of the European settler and the native overlord. Up to that time the superiority of the latter had never been disputed by either French or English. The representatives of both nations had been content to be the vassals of the Nuwáb of the Karnátik. The battle of

St. Thomé effected a revolution in this respect. To Europeans and Natives alike it was as the storming of the Bastille. Thenceforward the alliance of the Europeans came to be eagerly sought by every pretender to dominion. The revolution had been effected by the genius of Dupleix. To him it opened new visions, illimitable plans of dominion. It had revealed to him how he could bring Southern India entirely under French influence. It was only requisite that the war with England should continue, and that he should have a free hand. The rest he would care for.

CHAPTER IV

THE FLAW IN THE MACHINE

DUPLEIX had everything within his power. He had Pondichery, Kárikál, and Madras. He had inspired the Nuwáb with a wholesome dread of French prowess. The English, to the number of about 200, all told, had taken refuge in Fort St. David, a fort purchased by the East India Company in 1691, close to the native town of Gudálur, sixteen miles south of Pondichery. The fort was not strong, and a bold effort, well directed, could have secured it, for Dupleix could put into the field at least 900 Europeans.

Dupleix had many brilliant qualities. He was a great organiser, could take a comprehensive and accurate view of the political situation; was thoroughly acquainted with the weak and the strong points of his position. But there was one flaw in his organisation. He was not a man of action. He did not possess the power, granted in a marvellous degree to the man who was soon to become his chief opponent, of personally directing operations in the field. At the moment at which we have arrived he recognised that there was but one thing to be done to complete the destruction of the English, and that was to drive them from Fort St. David. Their expulsion would complete the work begun at Madras. It presented no difficulties, for he outnumbered his enemy in the proportion of about five to one.

He saw as clearly as we, looking back, can see it now, that it was the one thing to be done. Not for an instant did he hesitate. He organised a force of 900 Europeans, 600 trained sipáhis, 100 Africans, with six field-pieces and six mortars, to march against the place. Then came the question of command. He had at least one capable officer at his disposal, the Paradis who had triumphed at St. Thomé. But Paradis was only a captain, and the senior officers insisted on their rights. In an evil hour Dupleix recognised the force of their arguments, and confided the command of the expedition to an incapable octogenarian named de Bury. De Bury marched against Fort St. David the 19th of December, crossed the Panár river the following morning, took possession of a walled garden, and allowed his troops to disperse to cook their dinners, without placing sentries of any kind. There they were surprised and compelled to a hasty and disorderly flight by the native troops of the Nuwáb of the Karnátik, led by his two sons,—the very troops whom 230 of them had beaten but seven weeks before.

This was a blow, though not an irreparable blow. To minimise its effects Dupleix reopened negotiations with the Nuwáb, who, he had some reason to believe, was anxious for an accommodation. He found the Nuwáb not indisposed to come to an arrangement, provided only that Fort St. George were transferred to his keeping. To bring the negociation to an issue, one way or another, Dupleix resolved to surprise Fort St. David by an attack from the sea-side. For this purpose he embarked 500 men in country boats, and sent them to the attack (January 10). But the elements were adverse. A storm came on, which compelled the boats to return.

But the blind goddess was not even then wearied. She gave him another chance, and a great one. Ten days after the fruitless boat expedition a French squadron of four ships, under Commodore Dordelin, arrived off the coast. It would seem that a combined attack by sea and land on the English fort could not have failed. It is difficult to say why it was not attempted. Possibly the solution is to be found in the nerveless character of Dordelin, and in the fact that, on the seas, he was not subject to the orders of the Pondichery Council. The appearance of the squadron off the coast had, however, the effect of bringing the Nuwáb to terms. He had never much cared for the English, and believing that they were abandoned by their countrymen, whilst the French had the support of four ships of war; dreading moreover lest the French should seriously threaten him in the province of Arcot, he renounced his claims on Madras, and signed with Dupleix a treaty in which he confirmed the French in the possession of the territories they actually held. This treaty was ratified by his son, Máphúz Khán, in person (February 1748).

Now, at last, Dupleix had the opportunity which a bold stroke might have made decisive. A well-directed attack on Fort St. David, supported by the ships, could not have failed. The garrison had no longer the army of the Nuwáb to depend upon. But the blow, to be successful, must be struck at once. The English squadron was in the Húglí, waiting only for reinforcements, now overdue, to sail down to the succour of their countrymen. In war the opportune moment can never be allowed to pass with impunity. But, on this occasion, Dupleix did unaccountably allow it to slip. Without any protest on his part, indeed, it would seem with his full concurrence, Dordelin, after the signature of the treaty with the Nuwáb, sailed for the western coast (February 19). Possibly he dreaded lest the northerly winds then prevailing might bring down upon him the English squadron whilst he was engaged before Fort St. David.

When the squadron had left, Dupleix, whose mind always recognised what ought to be done, organised a new expedition against Fort St. David. With the consent of the superior officers he confided the command to the capable Paradis. That officer set out March 13, crossed the Panár, took possession of the walled garden from which de Bury had been so precipitately expelled, and made his preparations for attack the following morning. But Fortune, who had granted Dupleix so many opportunities, who had given him the whole period from December 10 to the first week in March in which to make the attack with a certainty of success, gave sudden evidence that she was not to be trifled with with impunity. Twenty-four hours probably, forty-eight certainly, would have made all the difference, for Fort St. David could not have offered a serious resistance to a daring attack. But when the morning of the 14th of March broke, Paradis beheld the sea facing Gudálur covered with ships bearing the flag of England, and having on board a reinforcement of a hundred men for the garrison of the threatened fort. Recognising that the English fleet was at once a succour to Fort St. David and a menace to Pondichery, he retraced his steps to the camp near that town, and a few days later, when the English fleet appeared before it, entered the town itself. Dupleix had recognised that he, who had planned the expulsion of the English, might have to exert all his resources to ward off the counter-blow which the islanders were about to deliver.

But fortune gave him one more chance. The opportune arrival of a French squadron drew off the English fleet, and Dupleix, thoroughly alive now to the value of time, resolved to strike one more blow for Fort St. David. On the 27th of June he despatched a force of 1800 men, of whom 800 were Europeans, to capture that place. Who the commander was I have been unable to ascertain, but he must have been a rash and incapable man. There had arrived at Fort St. David, some six months before, an officer who is one of the splendid illustrations of British skill and daring in India, Major Stringer Lawrence, and he commanded in chief at the English fort. Deceiving the French commander by reports, which the latter accepted without due inquiry, he led him to make a careless attack on the strongest part of the fort, received him there with his full force, and compelled him to retreat, beaten, baffled, and humiliated, to Pondichery.

This was his last attempt on Fort St. David. A few weeks later Dupleix was called upon to defend Pondichery against a powerful English fleet under the command of Admiral Boscawen.

CHAPTER V

The English Besiege Pondichery

Despatches from France had warned Dupleix that an English force, escorted by an English fleet, more powerful than any which had till then appeared in the Indian seas, had quitted England in the preceding November. At the period at which we have arrived, the end of June 1748, it might arrive at any moment. Renouncing then, as I have stated, further attempts on Fort St. David, Dupleix devoted himself, with all the energy of his nature, to strengthen the defences of Pondichery. With the invaluable aid of Paradis he made of the small fort of Ariákupun, nearly two miles from the town, an almost impregnable outwork, whilst the defences of the town itself he completed in a manner such as to render them, if well defended, very formidable if assailed by any but a very superior force.

But the force conveyed by the ships of Admiral Boscawen was very formidable. The fleet itself was, including the ships in the Indian seas, composed of thirty vessels, of which thirteen were ships of the line. The land forces it carried numbered 1400. But Holland was at war with France, and that country had pledged herself to supply 120 men from the garrison of the Dutch settlement of Nágápatnam. The same power had supplied likewise six ships belonging to her East India Company, conveying 500 tried soldiers. Added to these a large proportion of the sailors of both fleets were available for land service. It was certain that the Admiral would be able to put in action against the town not less than 3720 Europeans, aided by more than 2000 natives, armed and drilled in the European fashion.

Against this overwhelming force, as it seemed to the defenders, Dupleix had in Pondichery and Ariákupum 1800 Europeans and 3000 sipáhis.

The combined fleets appeared off the coast on the 11th of August, and the land operations began on the 19th. They continued till the 17th of October.

The attack was conducted with great vigour, for the Admiral knew that it would be dangerous to stay off the coast after the second week in October. The operations against Ariákupum, which it was necessary to gain before Pondichery could be attacked, were conducted with the greatest energy. But the defence was in all respects equal to the attack. I have before me a journal of the daily operations of the defence, written by the Diwán of M. Dupleix, a native named Rangápoulé, full of interesting details. It would seem from this that to Paradis was intrusted the defence of Ariákupum; that he repulsed all the assaults made upon it by the besiegers up to the 30th of August; that on that date the English succeeded in exploding the powder-magazine with the effect of rendering Ariákupum no longer tenable; that Paradis and his troops succeeded in falling back on Pondichery, the siege of which really commenced the day following. Rangápoulé relates how, on the 11th of September,—not the 6th as stated by Mr. Orme,—Paradis was directed to make, and did make, a sortie at the head of from 800 to 900 men; how the native spy, who had given the information which had led Dupleix to decide on the sortie, led him into an ambuscade; how, suddenly assailed by a fire from his flank, Paradis was shot through the head and killed; how, despite this heavy loss of his best officer, Dupleix never despaired. So stoutly did he defend himself that Admiral Boscawen was slowly brought to the conclusion that it would be impossible to take the place before the monsoon should set in. Vainly did he bring up his ships as close as he dared to bombard the place. On the 13th of October he felt that he must retreat. On the 14th he called a council of war, and with the advice of its members, in which he concurred, gave the necessary orders to destroy the batteries, the provisions, the camp equipage, and to re-embark. On the 17th, the besieging force, the largest body of Europeans till then massed on Indian soil, broke up and retreated on Fort St. David, leaving behind it 1065 men, who had succumbed either to the enemy's fire or to sickness contracted during the siege. The loss of the French amounted to 200 Europeans and 50 natives.

From the journal I have quoted it would seem that it was on the 1st of October that Dupleix realised that the English must eventually raise the siege. Some prisoners he had taken revealed the losses and discouragement of the besiegers, the anger of their admiral. On the 6th, Dupleix had learned from a similar source that the besiegers were suffering from sickness, and that, as a last resource, Admiral Boscawen intended to bring up his ships to bombard the place: on the 7th, that the fire of twenty-one ships had been brought to bear, but that the cannon-balls had fallen short. Of the conduct of Dupleix on the following day when a heavier fire was brought to bear, the Diwán writes: 'What has become of the bravery of the English compared with that of the incomparable Dupleix? It has vanished like night.' On the 9th and 11th he records the damaging effect of the fire from new French batteries brought to bear on the English ships. On the 13th he states that deserters had brought news that the raising of the siege had been practically decided upon in consequence mainly of the near approach of the monsoon. On the 16th he records the realisation of all their hopes, and the despatch in pursuit of the retiring troops of a strong force of European and native cavalry and infantry: on the 17th, the celebration of a 'Te Deum' in honour of the occasion: on the 18th, the departure of the allied fleets.

The raising of the siege of Pondichery left the rival parties almost in the position in which they were before the siege had been thought of. The French had Pondichery and Madras, the English only Fort St. David and the adjoining town of Gudálur. The English troops in that fort had indeed been slightly increased in number, but, early in the following year (1749), the reception by Dupleix of reinforcements to the extent of 200 men restored to the French their considerable numerical superiority. Dupleix was once more planning the reopening of operations against Fort St. David when he received information of the signing of the Peace of Aix-la-Chapelle, one clause of which necessitated the mutual restitution of conquests. With a bitter pang, then, he was compelled to restore to his late besiegers the Madras which he had gained by so much daring, and at the expense of breaking his intimate relations with the princes of the soil, a Madras much improved and strengthened. After five years of contest he found himself in the position, as far as possessions were concerned, in which he had been when he entered upon the strife. But his reputation, his prestige, and the reputation and prestige of his countrymen, had enormously increased. That of the English, by the capture of Madras, by their striking failure before Pondichery, had proportionately diminished. There can be no doubt but that, at this time, the French stood far higher in the estimation of the native princes and people than did their rivals. It was clear to Dupleix, even when he restored Madras, that this higher prestige would stand him in good stead in the contests which, despite the Treaty of Aix-la-Chapelle, he saw looming in the future. For his keen perception had convinced him that the hatred between the two European nations, once more face to face on the Coromandel coast, would be restrained from action by no paper convention arrived at in Europe.

CHAPTER VI

THE ZENITH OF HIS SUCCESS

WHEN the Peace of Aix-la-Chapelle forced the representatives in southern India of the two rival nations to revert to the position each had held before the outbreak of the war, and to exchange promises of amity, the results of the revolution which the victory of Paradis at St. Thomé had brought about became at once apparent. Before that battle had been fought the French and English had been alike regarded as simple traders. Subsequently to St. Thomé, they were looked upon as warriors of a very superior order, whose assistance in quarrels between rival pretenders would bring victory to the pretender whose cause they might be induced to espouse. This feeling especially prevailed with regard to the French, whose capture of Madras and whose repulse of the English from Pondichery had given them a very high prestige. It was impossible, so long as the two nations were openly at war, that the native princes should utilise their superior prowess in the manner indicated. But no sooner had the Peace of Aix-la-Chapelle ensured a nominal peace between them on Indian soil, than several native princes began to cast about how they could induce the chiefs of the two establishments to espouse their cause. One circumstance contributed largely to the success of the idea which these chiefs cherished. The treaty had left the French and English in southern India with a far greater number of European troops at their disposal than were required for a peace establishment. Unless they could profitably employ some of these, the respective Governors of Pondichery and Madras, of Pondichery especially, would be reduced to considerable straits to meet the expenditure thereby caused. It was likely, then, that any proposal from a native prince of position made to Dupleix to hire the superabundant troops at his disposal, either for payment in money or a grant of territory, or for both combined, would meet with a ready assent. The reader will have seen that the battle of St. Thomé had produced upon his mind an effect greater even than it had produced on the minds of the princes of the soil. It had opened out a vista of supremacy scarcely bounded by the Vindhyan range. He had already, in his imagination, so manipulated the native princes as to acquire, first, a supreme influence; secondly, supreme power, south of that range. He had felt quite certain that, sooner or later, his assistance would be implored. Already he had intimate relations with influential chiefs, and he knew, far better than his rivals knew, how to work their passions to the development of his idea. Added to this, he had at his disposal a larger number of European troops than the English could muster; he had trained, on the European model, a considerable number of sipáhis, and he had, serving under him, a small but select body of Maráthá horse. He was thus as ready to meet any demands the native chiefs might present to him, as these were to make them.

Nor were the English less ready, though from an entirely different cause. They cherished no ideas of supreme influence and supreme authority in southern India. But they were a practical people. They had a superabundance of soldiers. There were many places on the coast the possession of which would open out to them great facilities for the extension of their trade. They were as willing therefore as were the French to lend their soldiers for a consideration. But it must be borne in mind that whilst, in the case of the French, the main consideration was the increase of political influence and political power, in that of the English it was extension and expansion of commerce

It happened that whilst the rival nations were thus eager to lend their troops, the state of southern India was such that there was likely to be a multiplicity of borrowers. And as it was evident that the two people would not lend their men to the same prince, it followed that the moment the applications should be complied with, the French and English would be arrayed in arms against one another, as completely, though not as avowedly, as though no Treaty of Aix-la-Chapelle had ever been signed.

In June, 1748, whilst the French and English were combating in the vicinity of Pondichery and Fort

St. David, the Subáhdár of the Deccan, Nizám-ul-Mulk, had died, leaving a numerous family. Of his sons and grandsons only one was regarded as having immediate pretensions to succeed him. This was Muzaffar Jang, the son of a daughter, whom he had nominated himself. His eldest son was filling a high office at the court of Delhi; his second son, Nádir Jang, was a debauchee whom he had disinherited; and his three younger sons were in the harem. The rights of Muzaffar Jang to the succession had been confirmed by an Imperial farmán from the Emperor.

But, at the moment of the decease of the Subáhdár, the nominated heir was absent at Bíjápur, whilst the disinherited Nádir Jang was on the spot. The latter, disregarding his father's will and the farmán of the Emperor, seized his father's treasures and had himself proclaimed Subáhdár. Muzaffar Jang had at first the idea of invoking the assistance of the Maráthás, and proceeded for this purpose to the court of Puná. There he met Chandá Sáhib, son-in-law of the Dost Alí who had been Nuwáb of the Karnátik, and who, taken prisoner some eight years before by the Maráthás, had been kept since a prisoner from inability to pay the ransom demanded. Chandá Sáhib was personally allied with the French. Dupleix had received and protected his wife and family at Pondichery, where they still resided. The two princes soon became friends, and, acting on the advice of Chandá Sáhib, Muzaffar Jang opened negotiations with Dupleix. He represented to him that there were at

Puná two princes, one the legitimate heir to the *masnad* of the Deccan, the other to the office of Nuwáb of the Karnátik, and that they felt sure that with his powerful aid they might recover the positions which were their due. At the moment Dupleix was too much occupied with the English to respond satisfactorily to their requests, but no sooner had the conditions of the Peace of Aix-la-Chapelle been carried out in India, than he took the matter into most earnest consideration. He saw at a glance that a favourable response to the two suppliants would procure for him the very opening he required; that, if by his means, Muzaffar Jang were to become Subáhdár of the Deccan, and Chandá Sáhib Nuwáb of the Karnátik, the two most powerful princes in southern India—for Haidar Alí had not then raised Mysore to the position it attained under his tutelary genius—would become as French in all their sympathies, in all their actions, as though they were ruled from Pondichery. He recognised, in fact, in the applications from Puná the first step towards the realisation of his far-reaching dream.

No sooner, then, were his hands free than he guaranteed to the Peshwá the payment of the ransom of 700,000 rupees on behalf of Chandá Sáhib, and promised both to that prince and to Muzaffar Jang all the assistance which Pondichery could furnish them in the carrying out of their schemes. Released from captivity, Chandá Sáhib marched with a body of 3000 men he had levied towards the Karnátik, having entered into an agreement with Dupleix whereby he was to receive the aid of 2000 sipáhis, drilled in the European fashion, and 400 Frenchmen. When he reached the frontier his own levies had increased to 6000. There he was joined by Muzaffar Jang at the head of 30,000 men. Towards the end of July the French auxiliaries, to the number stipulated, commanded by Bussy, afterwards to become very famous, and by d'Auteuil who had distinguished himself at the defence of Pondichery, found him at the Damálcherrí Pass in the district of North Arcot. There they learnt that the actual Nuwáb, Anwár-ud-dín, the same who had disputed the right of the French to retain Madras, was with his two sons and a force of 20,000 experienced soldiers, aided by sixty European adventurers, waiting for them at Ambur, in the same district. On Ambur, then, they marched, sighted the Nuwáb's army on the 3rd of August, attacked it, and obtained a complete victory. In the heat of the battle Anwár-ud-dín was slain; the eldest son, Maphuz Khán, was taken prisoner; the younger, Muhammad Alí, destined to become famous through the championing of his cause by the English, fled as fast as he could ride to Trichinopoli.

The battle was decisive. The two princes supported by Dupleix became, in consequence of it, masters of all the Karnátik, save Trichinopoli. There remained, however, in addition to Trichinopoli, Nádir Jang to be reckoned with. That prince was in the field at the head of a considerable army. The question which presented itself to the two allies was whether they should march at once against him, or on Trichinopoli, thence to expel, if they could not capture, Muhammad Alí. They decided on the latter course. Between decision and execution, however, there was a very wide difference. Instead of marching direct on Trichinopoli, Chandá Sáhib wasted a considerable time in assuring himself of his new dignity, then, accompanied by Muzaffar Jang, proceeded to pay a ceremonious visit to Pondichery. Dupleix received them with the most brilliant display, and completed the conquest already more than half achieved of their hearts. The gratitude of Chandá Sáhib was unbounded. He conferred upon Dupleix the sovereignty of eighty-one villages adjoining the French possessions, and made promises of still more substantial donations. Muzaffar Jang was not less lavish of promises, though for the moment he had little to bestow, for Nádir Jang was in possession. He stayed at Pondichery eight days; negotiated a treaty with Dupleix for the furnishing him with an auxiliary force of Frenchmen, and then set out to join his army. Chandá Sáhib, whose family Dupleix had protected at Pondichery during the siege, remained, partly on their account, but mainly to concert measures with Dupleix.

It was, indeed, a decisive moment in the fortunes of Chandá Sáhib. The district of which the famous fort of Trichinopoli was the capital adjoined the South Arcot district, and, in those days, formed a portion of the territories of the Nuwáb of the Karnátik. The battle of Ambur had assured to Chandá Sáhib all the remainder. Of the districts which he claimed Trichinopoli alone remained unconquered. He knew the place well, for he had defended it against the Maráthás, and his surrender of it had cost him seven years of captivity. Dupleix was very urgent with him to march upon it without delay. Until he had it, he told him, he could not reckon on maintaining his position. It was above all necessary that the Karnátik should be cleared of foes before the greater enterprise against Nádir Jang should be undertaken. The remonstrances on the part of Dupleix against delay were very urgent indeed. There were, however, circumstances which seemed to Chandá Sáhib so full of the possibilities of danger on the one side, and so replete with temptations on the other, that he long hesitated as to the course he should follow. To enable the reader to judge tho position I must recount the action of the English, during the period just covered by the story.

I have stated that the Peace of Aix-la-Chapelle had found the English, scarcely less than their rivals, with a plethora of soldiers. A tempting offer made to them by a pretender to the throne of Tánjore to cede to them the town of Devikota, advantageously situated on the coast 120 miles south of Madras on the Kólrun, the great northern artery of the Káveri, and to pay all the expenses of the war, was eagerly grasped at, and in April, 1749, Captain Cope had been despatched with 430 English soldiers and 1000 sipáhis to seat the pretender on the coveted throne. Cope, after having been delayed on his way by a terrible storm, had reached the northern bank of the Kólrun, and had thence descried the reigning Rájá's army, ready, not so much to dispute his passage as to entice him into the difficult country beyond it. Cope, however, had no intention of indulging their fancies. His orders were to get possession of Devikota. On that place accordingly he marched, expecting to be supported by Admiral Boscawen, whose fleet was still off the coast. But the same storm which had delayed his march had greatly damaged the English fleet, and when Cope arrived within a mile of Devikota not a ship was to be seen. Cope, whose character was not enterprising, after vainly cannonading the place, retreated on Fort St. David. But the English had set their hearts on Devikota. They therefore despatched a fresh force of 800 British troops and 1500 sipáhis under the command of the capable Stringer Lawrence with instructions to take Devikota at any price. Lawrence stormed Devikota, and, throwing over the pretender on whose behalf the English had been nominally acting, made arrangements with the ruling prince for its permanent cession to the English Company.

It was about this time that Mr. Floyer, the Governor of Madras, received tidings of the battle of Ambur and its consequences. It seemed to him that he had no choice but to recognise the prince in possession.

and he accordingly recognised Chandá Sáhib. But when he heard of the march of the new Nuwáb on Pondichery, and of his reception there, and when about the same time he received imploring requests from Muhammad Alí urging him to espouse his cause, he hesitated for a moment whether he should recall his recognition. Admiral Boscawen, smarting under his repulse from Pondichery, promised to remain off the coast with his fleet, if he would return a favourable reply to Muhammad Alí. But the risk was too great. Floyer did not care to pledge all the resources of the Presidency to the cause of a man who had apparently but a very slight following. He refused therefore the Admiral's offer. Boscawen then quitted the coast with his ships (November 1).

Chandá Sáhib had felt nervous and ill at ease so long as Boscawen remained off the coast. But no sooner had information reached him that the English fleet had sailed, than, quite relieved from his fears, he set out from Pondichery with an army 20,000 strong, accompanied by Muzaffar Jang, and aided by 800 Frenchmen, 300 Africans, and a train of artillery, in the direction of Trichinopoli.

Had Chandá Sáhib only kept in view the one aim carefully instilled into his mind by Dupleix, he would have carried into action that great principle of the capable general, and have concentrated upon the decisive point of the campaign a force large enough to overcome all opposition. Had he marched, that is to say, directly on Trichinopoli, that place, feebly garrisoned by native troops, could not have offered a successful resistance. Dupleix had recognised this, and, counting on the carrying out of the plan he had carefully prepared, he regarded the departure of his guest's army for Trichinopoli as decisive of the war. His anger, rage, and disappointment may therefore be imagined when he received information, first, that Chandá Sáhib had turned away from the road to Trichinopoli, to attack Tánjore; and, secondly, that when he had arrived before that place, instead of attempting a surprise which could scarcely have failed, he had entered into negotiations with its Rájá, thus giving time to that prudent prince to strengthen his defences and to send to Nádir Jang for assistance. Angry as he was at the divergence from his plans, Dupleix recognised but one mode of repairing the mistake, and that was to assault and capture the place. He despatched instructions, then, to Duquesne, who commanded the French contingent, in that sense, and to Chandá Sáhib, the most urgent request to support the attack with his whole force. The assault made in consequence of these instructions reduced the Rájá to extremity. He hauled down his flag, and submitted to the onerous terms, limited chiefly to a large money payment, imposed upon him. But when the terms had been agreed to he put in action every wile of which he was master to delay the handing over of the coin, sending messengers to Nádir Jang to hasten his march. Chandá Sáhib, despite the pressing entreaties of Dupleix, allowed himself to be cajoled. He was detained by promises before Tanjore until Nádir Jang had entered the Karnátik. Then, thoroughly aroused, he would have attempted to storm the town; but his troops, alarmed by the near approach of Nádir Jang, not only refused to follow him, but broke up without orders, and fell back on Pondichery.

This was a blow which for the moment shattered the plans of Dupleix. The position, indeed, was now inverted. For, whereas, but a few weeks before, his ally had possessed all the Karnátik except Trichinopoli, the whole of that province had now fallen into the hands of Nádir Jang, who, with an enormous army, estimated at 300,000 men, had arrived at Valdávur, just nine miles from Pondichery. The English, too, had now recognised Muhammad Alí as the true Nuwáb, and that prince was likewise present. A few days later, April 2, Major Lawrence, with 600 Englishmen under his command, joined Nádir Jang.

The occasion was one to test to the very core the stuff that was in a man. The weapons of Dupleix had broken in his hand, not from any fault or want of skill on his part, but because the weapons themselves were defective. It is not the fault of the swordsman if his sword-blade suddenly snaps; nor of the infantry soldier if his bayonet bends in the thrust. Chandá Sáhib had snapped like the sword-blade, and, at the moment, all the French superior military officers were bending bayonets. Duquesne had died before Tanjore.

Goupil, who had succeeded him, was incapacitated by illness. The next officer, D'Auteuil, a good officer in a secondary position, was totally unfitted to lead in chief. Yet on this occasion, for want of a known better man, it was necessary to employ D'Auteuil. It would never do, argued Dupleix, to sit quietly in Pondichery, as if overawed, in the presence of an enemy within nine miles of the capital. There was but one mode, his long experience told him, of meeting Asiatics, and that was to affront them in the field. He could muster 2000 French soldiers and a respectable force of sipáhis, and the troops of Chandá Sáhib and of Muzaffar Jang were there. Upon this principle, then, he would act. Accordingly he despatched all the troops at his disposal, except a few for the routine duties, with instructions to take up a position opposite to that of the enormous force of Nádir Jang, and, if occasion should offer, to attack it. Meanwhile, he endeavoured, by the means at which he was an adept, to win over Nádir Jang to French interests.

Again did his weapon break in his hand. D'Auteuil, who commanded the French contingent, had planned a surprise of the enemy when, on the eve of the night on which he had decided to strike the blow, his officers announced to him that neither they nor their men would follow him. The unfortunate issue of the attempt on Tanjore, and the disappointment engendered by the failure to receive the promised prize-money there, had produced a discontent so deep-seated as to determine the officers and men not to fight. Nay more, they insisted on retreating. This they did during the night, leaving eleven guns and forty men behind them. Chandá Sáhib accompanied them, commanding the rear-guard to cover the retreat. Muzaffar Jang surrendered to the tender mercies of his uncle, who promptly had him handcuffed and placed in confinement.

The retreat was not a very happy one. It was discovered early in the morning, and the Maráthá horse, dashing in pursuit, caught up the demoralised army before it had entered Pondichery, and killed nineteen Frenchmen. The forty who had been left behind met the same fate.

'It is easy to imagine,' writes Dupleix in his Memoirs, 'what was the mortification of Dupleix[1] when he was informed of all the details of the conduct of our cowardly officers, and further, to complete his misfortunes, that Muzaffar Jang had been taken prisoner and placed in irons by Nádir Jang.' But never was Dupleix greater than when confronted by difficulties which would have overwhelmed ordinary men. The arrival of the fugitives had given him the first intimation of the discontent which had produced the mutiny. In the crisis, he behaved with a vigour and an energy which produced the best results. He placed D'Auteuil under arrest for retreating without orders, the officers who had been the ring-leaders he brought to trial, the men he addressed in a tone and in a manner which speedily brought them to a condi-

[1] Dupleix wrote in the third person.

tion of shame and repentance. They implored to be allowed an opportunity of recovering their good name. Whilst thus dealing with his troops, he sent two envoys to treat with Nádir Jang. With that prince his tone was as haughty as though it were he who was dictating terms. He demanded that no one of the family of Anwáru'-dín should be recognised as Nuwáb of the Karnátik, and that to the children of Muzaffar Jang should be given the estates of their father. Whilst thus openly asserting himself, he sent skilled native diplomatists to intrigue with some of the most powerful nobles in the camp of Nádir Jang. The result of their efforts will appear in due course.

Nádir Jang refused the propositions of Dupleix. But his emissaries, who had been seven days in the camp of the Subáhdár, had not been idle. He himself had employed those seven days in the reorganisation of his army. Some officers had been reduced. Others had expressed the most fervent contrition. The men were eager to wipe out the memory of their misconduct by brilliant service. D'Auteuil had completely vindicated himself, and had been restored to command. Among the officers of the force, Dupleix had especially marked the bearing and action of a young major named De la Touche, and he had resolved to trust him with command. His design was to surprise the camp of Nádir Jang, and, in concert with the nobles his emissaries had gained, to restore the vanished prestige of Pondichery. The duty was entrusted to De la Touche. That brilliant young officer set out with 300 Frenchmen the night after the return of the envoys from Valdávar, surprised the camp about three o'clock in the morning, and returned to Pondichery before the paucity of his numbers could be perceived. His men had killed 1200 of the enemy, and had lost but three of their own number. But the blow had had all the effect Dupleix had hoped from it. It so frightened the Subáhdár that he made a hasty retreat on Arcot, whilst Lawrence fell back with his English on Fort St. David.

By the retreat of Nádir Jang, Muhammad Alí was left without support, close to the fortified pagoda of Tíruvádí, some thirteen miles from Fort St. David. D'Auteuil, making a night march with 500 men, seized that fortified pagoda ; and, placing in it a garrison of seventy men, of whom twenty were French, established himself firmly on the Panár. Muhammad Alí, alarmed, sent pressing messages alike to Nádir Jang and the English for aid. The former sent him 20,000 men, the latter a detachment of 400 Englishmen and 1500 sipáhis under Captain Cope. It happened that the Governor, Mr. Floyer, had been removed from his office, and Major Lawrence had been ordered to take his place, pending the arrival of the new Governor, Mr. Saunders, from Viszagatam. He had no choice, therefore, but to send Cope in command.

Thus strengthened, Muhammad Alí marched against Tíruvádí. Alarmed by the formidable appearance it presented, he turned then to the French camp, and cannonaded the position taken up by D'Auteuil. But that officer was on the alert, and replied so warmly that the assailants, after losing many men, fell back discouraged. During their retreat a difference of opinion broke out between the two leaders, which culminated in the return of the English to Fort St. David, and in the encamping of Muhammad Alí, desirous of persuading the English to accompany him to Arcot, on the Panár, between Tíruvádí and Fort St. David, the river in his rear.

Not a born soldier, nor gifted with the divine power—possessed in the highest degree of perfection by the rival who was to thwart all his plans—of carrying into execution plans suggested by his genius, Dupleix recognised on the instant the falseness of the position taken by Muhammad Alí, and he resolved to make him pay the penalty. Accordingly, he sent orders to D'Auteuil to break up his camp and move on Tíruvádí. There, he told him, he would be joined by 1200 Frenchmen and 2500 sipáhis led by De la Touche, and by 1000 horse under Chandá Sáhib. At the head of the combined force he was to march at once to surprise Muhammad Alí. D'Auteuil carried out his orders to the letter; stormed on the 1st of September the camp of the pretender, though defended by 20,000 men, and drove the enemy in headlong flight towards Gingi. Muhammad Alí, followed by two attendants only, fled to Arcot. The loss of his followers was considerable. The French did not lose a single man.

D'Auteuil, instructed by Dupleix, followed up the

blow. Bussy was detached to march on Gingi, a town and fortress fifty miles distant, considered the strongest in South Arcot, and believed to secure to its possessor the command over that province. The natives regarded it as impregnable, for it had baffled even the famous Síváji. Against this place Bussy marched on the 3rd of September with 250 Frenchmen and 1500 sipáhis, arrived within three miles of it on the 11th, defeated the troops in front of it, the remnants of the army of Muhammad Alí, the same day; and, following up his victory, gained the town before nightfall. There remained still the strong fortress, which consisted of citadels on the summits of three steep mountains, covered by a cordon of advanced works. Waiting till the moon should have hidden her light, Bussy, with three picked detachments, escaladed these simultaneously, and won them. As the day broke, his men had just gained the last citadel. It was a splendid performance, the like of which had never before been witnessed in India.

It made a great impression. It roused Nádir Jang from the careless dissipation of his easy life. It terrified Muhammad Alí. It produced the general conviction that the French were irresistible. Nádir Jang had been just roused from his lethargy, when his terror was increased by the news that D'Auteuil was marching on Arcot. The next day brought him a letter from Dupleix, demanding the release of Muzaffar Jang and his restoration to the appointments he had held in his grandfather's lifetime, the recognition of Chandá Sáhib as Nuwáb of the Karnátik, and the cession to the French of the town of Masulipatam. The first of these conditions meant, the Subáhdár considered, the release of a man who would at once pose as a rival to himself. Rather than that, it was better to risk the result of war. Accordingly, he marched with an army of upwards of 100,000 men in the direction of Gingi. For about two months the operations of both armies were prevented by an unusually fierce rainy season. These months were employed by Dupleix in constant secret correspondence with the powerful chiefs who formed the backbone of Nádir Jang's army, and who, he well knew, bore him personally no good-will. Finally, before the rainy season had ended, he had entered into a convention with these, that if Nádir Jang should still refuse acceptance of the terms offered by Dupleix, they should turn against him in the crisis of the first battle. Even the minor details, regulating the very moment of their defection, were carefully settled.

The inaction, forced upon him by the heavy rainy season, combined with the prospect of a long and hazardous campaign against an enemy so formidable as the French, produced a revulsion in the mind of Nádir Jang. So long as hostilities should last his presence in camp was necessary, and to a man of his sensual nature camp-life was an abhorrence. He wrote, then, early in December, to Dupleix, to offer to agree to the terms the latter had proposed three months earlier. Dupleix, regarding only the direct aim of all his negotiations—the establishment of French predominance in Southern India—and not very confident of the chances of war, wrote at once to D'Auteuil to suspend military operations pending the receipt of further instructions. But, meanwhile, a change had taken place in the command of the French auxiliaries. A severe attack of gout had compelled D'Auteuil to quit the army, and his place had been taken by the young and brilliant De la Touche. That officer had been careful to maintain the secret correspondence with the disaffected nobles of the Subáhdár's army which Dupleix had initiated. From these he learned the nature of the terms sent by Nádir Jang to Pondichery, and the assurance that they were not intended to be adhered to, and that it was advisable to act at once. Under the circumstances, De la Touche considered himself justified in acting upon his earlier instructions. Transmitting then a reply to Dupleix that his orders had arrived too late, for that he had arranged with his friends in the Subáhdár's camp to act that night (December 15), he set out at the head of 800 Frenchmen, 3000 sipáhis, and ten guns, for that camp. At four o'clock in the morning he sighted it, and attacked. At first, he carried all before him. But, in the very crisis of the action, he noticed advancing towards his left flank a body of some 20,000 men. Were these enemies, he would be ruined, for retreat was impossible. Very soon, however, he recognised the signal pre-arranged by the chiefs he had won over. The two armies joining, then made for the part of the field in which Nádir Jang was to be found. That prince, relying upon his dispatch to Dupleix, had not, at the first alarm, believed in the reality of the attack. When the fact could be no longer doubted, he took his station in the part of the field where his guns were posted, seated on his elephant. Near him, seated also on an elephant, but attended by an executioner who had orders to behead him on the first symptom of treason, was his nephew, Muzaffar Jang. Suddenly he noticed a falling back of his immediate troops, accompanied by a great commotion. He inquired the cause, and realising that some of his nobles had turned against him, he made a sign to the executioner to slay his victim. The man delayed; and, at the moment, the Nuwáb of Cuddapah, one of the leading rebels, approached the Subáhdár, shot him through the heart, and, having ordered an attendant to cut off his head, placed it at the feet of Muzaffar Jang.

For that prince, the protégé of Dupleix, the friend of Chandá Sáhib, there was thus an instant transition from a prison to a throne. He was at once recognised as Subáhdár of the Deccan. There was not a man in the army of his uncle who did not at once transfer to him his allegiance. Bussy, who had been sent by De la Touche to convey his congratulations, found the recent prisoner sitting in state surrounded by his nobles. When, the same evening, De la Touche paid his respects in person, Muzaffar Jang announced to him his intention of proceeding at once to Pondichery, to obtain the advice of the illustrious man who ruled there.

To Dupleix the news of the victory had come as a startling but most welcome surprise. He had not dared to hope for it, so impossible had it seemed to him. Yet it was in very deed the direct result of his own policy. He had first stretched out the hand to Muzaffar Jang. He had organised the conspiracy against his uncle. For a moment, so dark appeared the prospects of Muzaffar Jang, he was inclined to make terms with that uncle. The daring of De la Touche had saved him from that error. And now, his policy was triumphing all along the line. A French protégé was Subáhdár of the Deccan. A French protégé would soon become Nuwáb of the Karnátik. The English, without a leader, for Lawrence had left for England, and the superlative merits of Clive had not as yet been discovered, were crouching at Fort St. David. Their ally, Nádir Jang, was dead. Their protégé, Muhammad Alí, had, after many difficulties, succeeded in reaching Trichinopoli, but without a following. Never had policy triumphed more completely than had the policy of Dupleix.

The visit of the new Subáhdár to Pondichery only confirmed his power. The victory over Nádir Jang had brought vast riches to Pondichery, for the spoils were enormous. But those spoils were the least valued of the results. At the first formal meeting with Dupleix, Muzaffar Jang, in open darbár, conferred upon the French Governor the title of Nuwáb of the territories between the river Krishna and Cape Comorin, including Maisur and the entire Karnátik; he bestowed upon him as a personal gift the village of Valdávar, with the lands depending on it; he created him a Commander of Seven Thousand, one of the highest honours known under the Mughals; he directed that the French coins should be the recognised currency of Southern India; he confirmed the sovereignty of the French Company over Masulipatam and Yanáon, and finally assured Dupleix that he was the adviser to whom he would turn in all his political actions.

The conduct of Dupleix on this occasion was marked by a self-denial as politic as it was patriotic. Dupleix was not a self-seeker. His aim was the glory and interest of France. In negotiating with native princes he never allowed flattery or self-interest to turn him from the direct line of policy he had marked out. On this occasion he accepted with professions of gratitude the personal honours conferred upon him: he accepted for France the cession of territory about Masulipatam and Yanáon. But he did not, he felt he could not, accept the title of Nuwáb of the Karnátik. Leading forward Chandá Sáhib, he presented him to the new Subáhdár as an old and tried friend upon whom that honour had been already conferred, and solicited confirmation of it. His renunciation produced the very best effect. Chandá Sáhib was at once invested. But of the three principal actors present at that interview Dupleix emerged from it the most powerful in influence and prestige.

The battle gained by De la Touche had indeed enormously increased the power of the French. Muzaffar Jang paid to them no less than 1,000,000 rupees in hard cash, one-half of which represented the repayment of sums advanced. The territorial acquisitions represented an income of nearly 400,000 rupees annually. Then a proposal, one for which Dupleix had laid himself open and which he eagerly accepted, came from the Subáhdár, the effect of which was to relieve the strain on the finances of Pondichery, and to give the French a practical preponderance in the counsels of the Subáhdár at his capital.

This proposal took the form of a request that a body of French troops commanded by a capable officer should accompany the Subáhdár to his capital, to be paid from his treasury, and to be always at his disposal. Dupleix, recognising in this action a mode of retaining permanent influence at the Court of the Subáhdár, at once acquiesced, and, De la Touche having been invalided to Europe, nominated Bussy for the post. The result showed that he could not have made a better selection.

All arrangements having been made, Muzaffar Jang prepared to march to Aurangábád, which was at the time the favoured capital of the Subáhdárs. Bussy, commanding 300 Frenchmen and 1500 trained sipáhis, was to accompany him. The Subáhdár set out on the 7th of January,

1751. Bussy started two days later, and joined him on the 15th. Before the Subáhdár had left, Muhammad Alí had made overtures for the surrender, under certain conditions, of Trichinopoli. These conditions had been accepted. Chandá Sáhib remained thus apparently without rival or competitor.

The policy of Dupleix had triumphed. He had made French influence, not only preponderant, but predominant, in Southern India. Yet, within a few weeks a little cloud appeared on the horizon, which was dissipated only by the decision and the cannon of Bussy. The Nuwábs who had rebelled against Nádir Jang soon began to intrigue against his successor. But their treason was discovered, and Muzaffar Jang, calling upon Bussy to follow him, charged the rebel chiefs with his cavalry. The latter held their ground until the French came up. Then, in a few minutes, the rebels broke up, one of their leaders lying dead on the field, another, the Nuwáb of Cuddapah, grievously wounded. Him they attempted to carry off. But Muzaffar Jang, resolved that he should not escape, followed him. In the pursuit he came upon a third confederate, the Nuwáb of Karnúl. Between the two and their immediate followers a hand-to-hand contest ensued which terminated in the death of both, Muzaffar Jang being brained by a spear-thrust, and the Nuwáb cut to pieces.

The crisis was one which might have the gravest consequences for French interests. Had there been on the spot a pretender of ability and influence to take the place of the Subáhdár and to declare himself his successor; or, had Dupleix been represented on the spot by any other than a man of first-rate capacity and decision, it was quite upon the cards that the result of the fighting and intrigues of the previous twelve months might have been lost in an hour. But Bussy was a man of first-rate capacity. He possessed a clear brain, and an intuitive power of managing the natives of India. To think on the moment, to decide on the moment, to act on the moment—these were his maxims. On this occasion he recognised on the instant that all was likely to be lost unless he should take the lead. He took it on the moment. I have stated that when, in June, 1748, Nizám-ul-Mulk, the Subáhdár of the Deccan, died, he had left three younger sons in the harem. The names of these were Salábat Jang, Nizám Alí, and Basálat Jang. When Nádir Jang had taken possession of his father's territories, his first act had been to place these princes in confinement. They were still in confinement when Muzaffar Jang was killed. Bussy having decided to take the lead, the problem he had to solve was whether it was advisable in the interests of France to proclaim the infant son of Muzaffar Jang to be Subáhdár or to bestow the *masnad* on the eldest of his uncles. Recognising at a glance that in India minorities always give incentives to intriguers, he decided on the latter course. Hastily assembling the principal nobles present, he unfolded to them his proposal and the reason for it, and obtained from them general consent. That same day Salábat Jang was released from confinement and proclaimed Subáhdár of the Deccan. Again did Southern India witness a prompt transition from a prison to a throne.

Thus, by a happy act of audacity and decision, did Bussy retain for Dupleix all the advantages which he had gained from his support of Muzaffar Jang. He gained for him and for France others not less precious. One of the first acts of the new Subáhdár was to join to the French possessions at Masulipatam the territories depending on the towns of Nizámpatnam, of Kondavír, of Álamnává, and of Narsápur, in its vicinity. He rebuilt for him the factories of Yanáon; and he presented to Dupleix the town of Mafuz Bandar (Chicacole), in the Ganjám district. A few days later the new Subáhdár set his army in motion, traversed in triumph the territories of the rebel nobles, and finally entered Aurangábád, June 29. Here, in the presence of Bussy and the nobles of the province, Salábat Jang, in virtue of a farmán received from Delhi, was solemnly invested with the dignities appertaining to the office of Subáhdár of the Deccan. In him Dupleix possessed, to the last hour of his life, a true and admiring friend.

By the means related in this chapter Dupleix had, in the early days of 1751, brought French India to the height of its glory and power. Through Bussy and the Subáhdár his influence was supreme in the territories now known as the territories of the Nizám.

It was soon to become supreme in the territories called by the English the 'Northern Sirkars,' comprising Ganjám, Vizagapatam, Godávarí, and Krishná. It was supreme in the territories subsequently known as the 'Ceded Districts,' comprising Cuddapah, Karnúl, and Bellláry. Through Chandá Sáhib, it was equally supreme in the Karnátik, with the exception of Trichinopoli, held by Muhammad Alí, and of Tanjore, governed by its own prince. Excepted, too, must be Madras and Fort St. David, in which, however, at the moment, the English showed few signs of life. Apparently their influence had sunk to zero. For the moment, then, the astute ruler of Pondichery had triumphed all along the line. He could not detect the presence of the vestige of a cloud on the horizon. His one enemy, Muhammad Alí, had offered to come into his scheme. The English were inactive, and apparently hopeless of interfering wlth his plans. What was there, then, which could possibly prevent the successful development of his far-reaching schemes? He could detect nothing. The English equally could detect nothing. Yet, though they knew it not, there was brooding amid the silence of Fort St. David a man who did accomplish that apparently impossible feat.

CHAPTER VII

The English are roused to Action

The pretender to the Karnátik, supported by the English, had, we have seen, fled almost unattended to Trichinopoli. Thence, hopeless of success, he had made overtures to Dupleix, agreeing to recognise Chandá Sáhib as Nuwáb, and to surrender to him Trichinopoli and its dependencies, on condition (1) that the treasures left by his father should be restored to him; (2) that he should receive a subordinate province in lieu of the Karnátik. Dupleix had accepted these conditions, and had obtained from Muzaffar Jang a promise to carry them out. When, however, after the departure of Bussy and the Subáhdár from Pondichery, Dupleix pressed Muhammad Alí to perform his part of the agreement, engaging to place him at once in the position in which he had covenanted to place him, Muhammad Alí first hesitated, then asked for fresh guarantees. Meanwhile, he was imploring the English to come to his aid. For four months he implored in vain; but when, at the end of that period, he had wrung from them a promise of substantive assistance in the event of his being attacked, he boldly threw off the mask and informed

Dupleix that he was resolved to maintain Trichinopoli against him at all costs. This message decided Dupleix. Recognising the necessity of prompt action, he despatched, in the month of March (1751), D'Auteuil with 400 Frenchmen, a few Africans, and some guns, to accompany the force of Chandá Sáhib, from 7000 to 8000 strong, in its march to Trichinopoli, thence to expel Muhammad Alí.

But Mr. Saunders, who then directed English interests at Fort St. David, had been before-hand with him. Once resolved to succour Muhammad Alí, Saunders recognised the necessity of employing all his force for that purpose. Were Chandá Sáhib to take that place, there would be no limit to the development of the gigantic plans of Dupleix. Whilst then he had despatched, early in February, Captain Cope with 280 Englishmen and 300 sipáhis to assist Muhammad Alí within Trichinopoli, he prepared another body composed of 500 Englishmen, 100 Africans, and 1000 sipáhis, to be ready to act according as circumstances might require. When, then, D'Auteuil and Chandá Sáhib quitted Pondichery in March, in the manner and for the purpose already stated, Saunders despatched the troops he had organised to follow and to watch their motions. The English force was commanded by an officer of Swiss origin, named De Gingen.

The instructions given by Saunders to De Gingen were precise. He was to watch the movements of the enemy, but, recollecting the fact that France and

England were at peace, he was on no account to attack them until he should have been joined by the native levies of Muhammad Alí. When that junction should have been effected, the action of Muhammad Alí would cover, morally, the action of the English. This convenient fiction, practised by the French and English alike, permitted the representatives of two nations at peace in Europe to wage deadly and unremitting hostilities against each other in Southern India.

I propose to relate here only those salient actions of the rival field-forces which are necessary to the comprehension of the policy of Dupleix. It was at this period, and during the periods that followed, his misfortune to be badly served in the field. His best general was with the Subáhdár at Aurangábád, and could not be spared from thence. D'Auteuil was gouty and infirm, and had once before failed in his hands. But he had advices from France that the young and brilliant De la Touche, who had already given proofs of more than ordinary capacity, would sail that autumn from France with 700 tried men, and he might be expected some time in 1752. Law of Lauriston, who had done well at the siege, and who had on its conclusion proceeded home to recruit, was due at any moment. Pending his arrival it was scarcely possible, he thought, that D'Auteuil should make a mistake, if he would only obey orders.

But D'Auteuil did not obey orders. He had accompanied Chandá Sáhib but a few marches from

Pondichery when he yielded to the solicitations of the Nuwáb to turn aside from the road to Trichinopoli, and march into northern Arcot. The object of Chandá Sáhib was to obtain money and troops. He succeeded in both objects; but, oblivious of the cardinal fact that, in war, time is a main factor, he had succeeded at the cost of leaving Muhammad Alí and the English masters in the southern district, occupying various posts and becoming daily more capable of offering him a very solid resistance.

At length, his own levies raised to 17,000 men, Chandá Sáhib took the road to Trichinopoli, always accompanied by D'Auteuil. But the delay had been considerable, and it was not till the first week of July that he came in sight of Volkondá, a strongly fortified town thirty-eight miles to the north-north-east of Trichinopoli. In front of it, on the south-west face, apparently blockading it on that side, was the joint army of Muhammad Alí and De Gingen.

The English leader had been unable, in consequence of the non-arrival of the levies of Muhammad Alí, whose presence with him would alone legitimatise his action, to carry out the intentions of Mr. Saunders. When, at last, 1600 horsemen from Trichinopoli did reach him, led by the brother of Muhammad Alí, De Gingen moved forwards, captured the fortified pagoda of Vardáchalam, and then marched on Volkondá. He arrived before it on the 2nd of July and at once summoned it. But the Governor, who had not quite made up his mind as to the cause he should espouse, learning that Chandá Sáhib was approaching, declined every offer, however persuasive. Two days later, Chandá Sáhib and D'Auteuil arrived. Towards them, likewise, the Governor showed himself equally inexorable. For a whole fortnight matters continued in this position, the English lying encamped in a grove about a mile and a-half to the south-west of the town, the French four miles to the north of it, both parties bidding against each other with the Governor, each afraid to attempt force lest the display of it should induce the Governor to summon his rival to his aid. De Gingen was the first to lose his patience. On the 19th, he made all his preparations to storm the place; marched on it at nightfall, gained the out-works, but failing in his main attack, deferred further proceedings till the morning. But his action had decided the Governor. Irritated by the attempt made to force his hand, and dreading the result of the renewed attack on the morrow, he despatched an invitation to D'Auteuil to enter the town. The Frenchman complied on the instant. When then, early the following morning, De Gingen led his men to the assault, he was received by a well-directed fire from behind the walls of the town, whilst another fire, scarcely less formidable, poured upon his flank from the guns of the allied enemies, who had remained in the open. His men, panic-stricken by the cross-fire, so utterly unexpected, turned tail and fled; abandoning their native allies, and leaving one gun, several muskets, and their camp equipage in the hands of the victors.

Here was an opportunity! Had Dupleix, like his great rival, been endowed with the supreme faculty of a great commander and been present; had Bussy been there, or De la Touche; or had there been a man in command who possessed the ordinary instinct of the fighting soldier, the question of supremacy in Southern India would have been decided on that 20th of July. There was the English force, comprising, within 300, the entire troops at the disposal of the English Company, in full flight, having lost their guns, their camp equipage, their supplies, their retreat covered by a rabble of native cavalry, who would have dispersed at the first charge. Within a mile or two of them was the victorious French force, flushed with victory, at least equal in numbers, supported by 17,000 native troops commanded by the Nuwáb of the Karnátik in person. To settle the question of supremacy in Southern India it was requisite merely that the French commander should utter but one word—a word which inferior or timid commanders are always unwilling to utter—a word, nevertheless, which spoken when fighting against Asiatics has never been known to fail—the word 'Forward.' Let the reader realise the huddled mass of 500 Englishmen, 100 Africans, and 1000 sipáhis, hurrying from the field under the July sun of Southern India, panic-stricken and helpless, having abandoned everything. For the moment they were cowed, unable to listen to reason. Their leader was not much better: they all expected to hear the sound of the enemy's guns thundering in their rear. Had they heard that sound, they could scarcely have escaped destruction. Then, the French, marching rapidly on Trichinopoli, would probably have secured that fortress without a blow, and have firmly established their domination over Southern India.

Why did not D'Auteuil, who, an old soldier, must have known the great advantage to be ensured by pursuing a panic-stricken enemy,—why did not D'Auteuil utter that one word? The only answer that I can give is, that he was suffering at the moment from a severe attack of gout. It is a reason, but not an excuse, for his inaction. Excruciating as may have been his agony, he might have reasoned that Fortune is very jealous of her favours; that she does not often vouchsafe them a second time to the man who may have declined them when opportunely offered. But—he did not reason: he preferred, at this crisis of the fortunes of France in India, to remain idle; to permit the English to fall back towards that very Trichinopoli which it was his mission to secure, and which would thus be greatly strengthened by the addition to its garrison of the very men whom it had been in his power to destroy. Can we wonder that, a little later, it should be that very Trichinopoli which became the grave of the French?

But Fortune, pitying the condition of D'Auteuil, gave him a second chance. After a rest of twenty-four hours, the French commander felt himself well enough to follow, accompanied by Chandá Sáhib, in the direction taken by the English. A march of some twenty miles brought him to Utátur. There he beheld the English and their allies encamped in a position not only assailable, but so badly chosen that it would have been easy, with the superior native forces at his disposal, to cut them off from Trichinopoli. But instead of seizing promptly the favours offered by the blind goddess, D'Auteuil was content to dally with her. He took up a position not very far from the English camp, and endeavoured to entice them from their position. He so far succeeded that on the second day he drew a detachment of them into an ambuscade, and inflicted upon them no small loss. Encouraged by this, he arranged with Chandá Sáhib for an attack in force the day following. It was agreed between the two leaders that whilst Chandá Sáhib should lead the attack with clouds of cavalry the French infantry should follow it up and make it decisive. Here was an opportunity which, with ordinary care, might have atoned for the sluggishness after the rout of Volkondá. But, by some fatality, either Chandá Sáhib attacked too soon or the French came up too late, for the attack was repulsed. It had the effect, however, of convincing De Gingen that he could not with safety remain where he was. That night, therefore, he broke up his camp; and, marching for twelve hours, did not halt until he had reached the banks of the river Kólrun, facing Trichinopoli.

But, this time, D'Auteuil was on the alert. Six hours after De Gingen had quitted his position at Utátur, the French and their allies were on their track; and, marching as rapidly, encamped within three miles of them at eight o'clock that evening. The position of the English was full of danger. The country had declared for Chandá Sáhib, whose army was increasing every step, and here was De Gingen, encamped with dispirited troops, far fewer in number, on the northern bank of an unfordable river, within three miles of them. It was, moreover, still open to the enemy, by making a not very wide détour, to cut him off from the fortress. He resolved not to stay a single night in such a position. Risking an attack which, judging from the previous conduct of D'Auteuil, he felt confident would not be made, he collected boats, and before the next day had dawned, had crossed to Srírangam, a large island, fourteen miles by two, formed by the division of the Kolrún and the Káverí into two branches about eleven miles west of Trichinopoli. He did not consider himself safe even here, for, noting the preparations made by the French to follow him, he, on the night of the second day, crossed the Káverí and encamped under the walls of the fortress. D'Auteuil at once took possession of the island and attempted thence to bombard the fortress. But the distance, a fraction over two miles and a half, was too great. D'Auteuil then crossed the Káverí, and took post in front of the rock known as the French Rock, a mile and three-quarters to the east of the Fort Rock. He was there making preparations, the success of which he did not doubt, for the English were in the last stage of discouragement, when Dupleix, responding to his repeated requests, sent Law of Lauriston to relieve him. Law, whose conduct at the siege of Pondichery had attracted favourable attention, had but just returned from France, full of health and vigour. He was untried as a commander in the field, but his splendid conduct in a subordinate position had impressed the public with the belief that he would acquit himself well when he should hold the responsibility of command. Alas! It was the case of Berthier. The two positions require the possession of qualities widely differing. The general must be cool, careless of responsibility, ready to think and act on the moment. The subordinate need only be brave, prompt to execute the designs of another, intelligent enough to comprehend the drift of the orders he may receive. Law, excellently qualified to fill the second post, was of all the men who served Dupleix the most unfit for the first. He was hesitating, weak of purpose, vacillating, and fearful of responsibility. His first act on assuming command was to turn the siege into a blockade. Commanding, as he did, all the approaches to Trichinopoli from the Coromandel coast he believed it would be easier to starve out his enemy than to expel him.

Under ordinary circumstances his reasoning might have been sound. But in war a commander is bound to take into account the workings of time. Law had deliberately chosen the method which would require a period extending over months, and it was always possible that during those months events might occur to disturb his calculations. So it happened on this occasion. There had accompanied the English force to Volkondá, in the capacity of Commissary, a young writer of the English Company who had already, as a volunteer, given some proofs of conduct. This writer had been greatly disgusted with the leadership of De Gingen on the occasion of his attack on Volkondá. He had his own ideas as to the way war should be conducted. Regarding failure as certain, if the system then followed should be persevered with, he had quitted the force before it reached the Kolrun, and proceeded to Fort St. David to lay his plans before Mr. Saunders. The name of this officer was Robert Clive.

CHAPTER VIII

Robert Clive

Robert Clive was a young Englishman of the middle class who, born in 1725, and regarded by his relatives on his attaining manhood as utterly untractable, had been shipped off to Madras, in 1743, as a writer in the service of the East India Company. At Madras he had earned the character of being sullen, unsociable, and haughty; had on one occasion behaved with such marked insolence towards his superiors that he was compelled to apologise, and on another had attempted his own life. Prior to the attack on Madras by La Bourdonnais he would seem to have attached to himself but one friend. That friend was the Governor, Mr. Morse. Clive was aware that he had neglected his education in early life. Under the auspices of Governor Morse, he endeavoured to supply the deficiency by availing himself of the well-stored library which that gentleman was glad to place at his disposal.

When Madras surrendered to the French, Clive had fled in disguise to Fort St. David. When subsequently Boscawen laid siege to Pondichery he served as a volunteer with the besieging force, and, to use the words of a contemporary writer, 'by his gallant conduct gave the first prognostic of that high military spirit which was the spring of his future actions[1].' Subsequently, he accompanied Major Stringer Lawrence, also as a volunteer, in the attack on Devikota, 1749, and there, in the leading of the storming party, distinguished himself by his coolness and intrepidity. Referring subsequently to this period of his career, Major Lawrence, himself a man of remarkable ability and a distinguished soldier, thus wrote of his subordinate: 'A man of an undaunted resolution, of a cool temper, and a presence of mind which never left him in the greatest danger. Born a soldier, for, without a military education of any sort, or much conversing with any of the profession, from his judgment and good sense he led an army like an experienced officer, with a prudence that certainly warranted success. This young man's early genius surprised and engaged my attention, as well before as at the siege of Devikota, where he behaved in courage and judgment much beyond what could have been expected from his years, and his success afterwards confirmed what I had said to many people concerning him.'

For his conduct at Devikota Clive was transferred to the military service of the Company, and nominated Commissary to the Army. Very shortly after this nomination the break-down of his health compelled

[1] *Journal of the Siege of Pondichery*, republished in the *Asiatic Annual Register* for 1802. It is from this journal that Mr. Orme obtained his materials for that portion of his history.

him to take a sea-trip to the Hugli. On his return, in the cold season of 1751, he was directed to accompany as Commissary the force which was despatched under De Gingen to watch the action of Chandá Sáhib and the French, and the adventures of which I have told in the last chapter.

As Commissary of De Gingen's force, Clive had no influence in the direction of its operations. But that he highly disapproved of his superior's action is clear from the fact that he quitted the force to lay before the Governor of Fort St. David his reasons for the adoption of an entirely different system.

The Governor of Fort St. David, a fit associate of Stringer Lawrence, listened sympathisingly to the plan suggested by Clive. His fame has been overshadowed by the greater glory attaching to the name of the young counsellor who was explaining to him in the autumn of 1751 the plans which, properly carried out, would baffle all the hopes of Dupleix, but he was nevertheless a first-rate representative of that middle-class which won India for the Crown. A weaker man would have hesitated. My memory can recall hundreds of those I have met who would have absolutely refused to act on the suggestions of the young Commissary, for the situation was bristling with difficulties. Saunders had neither officers nor men at Fort St. David. His principal force was shut up in Trichinopoli, closely invested by an enemy superior in force, and subjected, or likely to be subjected, to all the horrors of famine. It was a positive necessity, then, that any troops which might arrive from England should be utilised for the despatch to the beleaguered fortress of the urgently required stores. Just at the moment a handful of troops arrived. These, 80 in number, accompanied by 300 sipáhis, Saunders despatched, in charge of stores, to Trichinopoli. A second small detachment was despatched under Captain Clarke, Clive accompanying him, to the same fortress. Both detachments succeeded in eluding the vigilance of the French and in joining their comrades. His visit to Trichinopoli only confirmed the ideas which had germinated in the mind of Clive. He found the garrison in the last stage of despondency, hopeless of relief, ready to surrender. He, a civilian just appointed officer, for he had been nominated Captain before quitting Fort St. David, had less than no influence with the commanders. There was nothing but contempt for the civilian who presumed to lecture soldiers on tactics. He returned, then, after the stay of a few days, to Fort St. David, to press more strongly than ever on Mr. Saunders the one plan which could save the English.

Saunders had already admitted the supreme force of the arguments of his young counsellor. At the time of Clive's previous visit he did not possess the necessary materials to act on them. But on the second, Clive found, to his delight, a garrison which, united to that at Madras, raised the number of troops, all told, to the total of 350. Some of these Saunders must retain for garrison purposes. Could he, himself a civilian, entrust the remainder to the charge of a young man, untrained in war, for the purpose of invading a province containing 1,500,000 inhabitants? It was to take upon his shoulders an enormous responsibility. To the lasting honour of Saunders, to the lasting advantage of his country, he did not shrink from that responsibility. By his orders, then, Clive set out from Madras, the 26th of August, 1751, with a force of 200 Englishmen, 300 sipáhis, and three small guns, to invade the province of North Arcot.

It would be foreign to the design of this book to relate the details of the wonderful march of Clive. It must suffice to state that he executed to the letter the plans which had suggested themselves to his daring mind. He captured Arcot, the capital of the Karnátik, and held it for fifty days against an army enormously out-numbering his own scanty levies alike in Europeans and natives. Not content with that, no sooner had he recognised that the siege had been raised, than he sallied forth in pursuit of the whilom besiegers, found them at Ární, attacked, and completely defeated them. Thence, having struck a blow which was felt throughout Southern India, he returned by way of Madras to Fort St. David, to concert further measures with Mr. Saunders.

Of all those who had felt the blow struck by the young Englishman, no one had realised its force so keenly as Dupleix. But it was the glory of that illustrious man that difficulties only incited him to prompt and energetic action. Reading, as clearly as

Clive himself, the full purport of the young Englishman's diversion, he had joined 100 Frenchmen to the force detached by Chandá Sáhib to retake Arcot. At the same time he sent every available Frenchman, down to the last recruit, and all his trained sipáhis, to strengthen Law before Trichinopoli. His hope was that whilst the force sent to Arcot should keep Clive and his following shut up, unable to aid the garrison, Law, pressing Trichinopoli hard, should force its surrender. With his force increased to 900 Frenchmen and 2000 trained sipáhis, with the army of the Nuwáb increased to 30,000 men, this was no impossible task for a resolute soldier. But Law, whilst he made a great show of activity, would not depart from the line he had laid down of a strict blockade. Bold in council, he was timid, suspicious, unenterprising himself, and checking enterprise in others in the field. Meanwhile, the arrival of troops from Mysore to the assistance of Muhammad Alí gave confidence to the garrison, and a few small outpost successes which followed so far raised their spirits that there was a talk of combining a general attack on the French. De Gingen, however, contented himself with despatching a party under Cope to storm the little post of Krishnávaram, about thirty miles from Trichinopoli, but recently occupied by the French and their allies. But in this attempt the English and their native allies were repulsed, and Captain Cope, who commanded the party, was mortally wounded.

Again, then, did matters look well for Law. Could

he only have made up his mind to risk a little, his superiority in numbers could scarcely have failed to prevail. Recognising this, Dupleix sent him, first entreaties, then commands. He told him that opportunities in war are rarely twice offered; that to strike whilst the enemy was reeling under his repulse from Krishnávaram was the true policy, the only policy. After much unnecessary hesitation, Law agreed, or seemed to agree; drew in his outposts, and made as though he would attack. But the responsibility was too great for his weak moral nature. At the critical moment he held back. Nor, when he received a despatch from Pondichery telling him that, to ensure him against molestation from Clive whilst he should be assailing Trichinopoli, Dupleix was threatening North Arcot and Madras, was he to be roused from his apathy.

The information furnished by Dupleix to Law was true. That great man, whose vision from the central point he occupied never deceived him, who ever recognised with the most perfect accuracy the thing which ought to be done, though he rarely possessed the men who would do it, had despatched 400 Frenchmen to strengthen the levies of Chandá Sáhib in Arcot, and the combined forces were at the moment eating up the country in the vicinity of Madras. To watch them, Clive, who had hoped to be sent to relieve Trichinopoli, was despatched with a few troops to Madras. Two days after his arrival there, reinforcements from Bengal landed. Having now at his disposal 380

Englishmen and 1300 trained sipáhis, he set out, February 22, 1752, to find his enemy. The latter, more numerous, for they counted 400 Frenchmen and 4000 natives, of whom 2500 were horsemen, had quitted the vicinity of Madras as soon as they had heard of Clive's arrival there, and had marched towards the fort of Arcot in the hope of surprising it. Failing in that attempt, they had doubled back, confident that Clive would soon be on their track, and, in the hope of enticing him into an ambuscade, had taken post at Káveripák, in a strong position, which Clive must traverse on his road to Arcot, and which he, with his impetuous nature, would, they calculated, reach after night had fallen. Their calculations had been made with the greatest accuracy. Clive fell into the trap; reached the position just as darkness was setting in, was completely surprised, was almost beaten; when, with the coolness and daring which characterised him, he took advantage of the darkness to attempt the strongest point of the hostile position, which, he thought, might have been left unguarded; succeeded, and changed a defeat into one of the most decisive victories ever achieved. The victory of Káveripák changed the position in Southern India. It cleared North Arcot of enemies, and enabled Clive to return to Fort St. David to take part, under Stringer Lawrence, in an expedition which was not only to relieve Trichinopoli, but to render that fortress and the country around it the grave of the soaring aspirations of Dupleix.

Truly had that prescient man foreseen the result of the timid action of Law. By his action in North Arcot, action which a mere accident, as he had the right to consider it, had caused to fail, he had procured for his general before Trichinopoli the time to make an assault which should be decisive. He could plead, he could implore, he could order, but he could not make Law fight. Not that Law was a coward. He had displayed his courage on many a field. It was the weight, the terrible weight, of moral responsibility which paralysed him. No man can be pronounced competent in action till he has been tried by that test. Under it, the Law who had been so brilliant when serving under another, was more useless than a child. To Dupleix, the weakness of his lieutenant caused a slow agony such as would have caused a man less buoyant to despair. What could he do with a man who had remained quiet whilst Káveripák was being fought, and who now, with Trichinopoli in front of him, was to be assailed by a fresh force led by the two most capable commanders the English possessed? He could not replace Law, for he had no one at his disposal. Bussy was at Aurangábád, D'Auteuil was still suffering, De la Touche was on the seas. There was, however, some hope of success if Law would but act. He occupied a central position, commanded the road from the coast; was well served by his native allies, and was still numerically stronger. If Law would but utilise these advantages, he might yet atone for the time wasted. Dupleix sent him then the most minute instructions, detailing the strength of the English force, the road it would take, the date of its departure, the fact that its movements would be encumbered by the necessity of escorting a large convoy, and then unfolded his plan. 'Leave,' he wrote, 'but a screen of troops before Trichinopoli; mass the remainder, and, marching eastwards, fall on the English relieving force with your superior numbers, and destroy it; then return, and make your decisive assault on the place.' To help him in this operation, which, in capable hands, had been perfectly feasible, he despatched from Pondichery every available Frenchman south of the Krishtna.

In the despatch of Dupleix to Law there shone the prescience of the statesman and the penetration of the real soldier. But the best plans, entrusted to incapable hands, will fail. So it was on this occasion. Instead of leaving only a screen before Trichinopoli, and marching with the bulk of his troops to crush Lawrence, Law kept the bulk of his men before the fortress, and sent the screen to accomplish that which the combined force would have found the toughest job on which they had ever been engaged. He failed, and he deserved to fail. Nor when, a day or two later, he ranged his troops in position and attacked Lawrence, was he more successful. The time, the position, the opportunity, were alike ill-chosen. The action was ill-fought, and the French had to fall back, disconcerted, on their Rock, whilst

Lawrence and his victorious men marched gaily into the fortress.

The reader who has studied the character of Dupleix, who has recognised the passionate desire by which he was animated to found an empire for France in Southern India, who has noted how, by every means except by that of actual presence in the field, he had laboured for that end, can picture to himself the anger and mortification of that great man when he realised that the inefficiency of Law had caused the failure of all his hopes. When he had recommended daring, Law had displayed an excess of caution. When he had shown Law how, by massing his strongest array against the enemy's weakest point, he could baffle that enemy, he had despatched his weakest array against the enemy's strongest point. This ineptitude had shattered for the moment all his plans. But it was a part of the nature of Dupleix never to despair so long as one hope remained. Glancing then at his position, he recognised that he was still strong with the Subáhdár of the Deccan. Bussy guided the councils of that prince. Nor, though Lawrence and Clive had relieved Trichinopoli, was it certain that they could do more than save that fortress. In numbers, the French and their allies still prevailed even there. The one thing he wanted was a man. It was clear to him that it would be a crime to trust Law any longer. But he had only D'Auteuil, just recovered from his attack of gout. He had had, he knew, reason to complain on a previous occasion of the slowness and caution of D'Auteuil, but he was neither so slow nor so cautious as Law had proved. Dupleix was yet deliberating as to the action he should take, when he received a despatch from Law which threw him into consternation. Law wrote that, despairing of success against Trichinopoli, he had resolved to retreat into the island of Srirangam. The idea of the timid Law in an island liable to be attacked from both banks of the river overwhelmed Dupleix. He recognised that in the presence of men like Lawrence and Clive he would be as a rat in a trap. He could bear anything but that. He sent then on the instant a peremptory order to Law to retreat, if he must retreat, not into Srirangam, but on Pondichery. To aid him, he used every effort to raise a force to second his efforts. By incredible exertion he collected 120 Europeans, and, adding to these 500 sipáhis and four field-pieces, he despatched them under D'Auteuil to take the road to Trichinopoli, effect a junction with Law, assume the command, and fall back on Pondichery.

But he had not yet realised the full measure of the incapacity of his lieutenant. The position occupied by Law before Trichinopoli was so strong, resting as it did upon two points which could not be turned, that even Lawrence and Clive regarded a direct attack upon it as hazardous. They thought, however, they might create an alarm which might have consequences, if they were to beat up the quarters of the native ally of the French, Chandá

Sáhib. They despatched Captain Dalton on this errand. Dalton, misled by a guide, found himself in the early hours of the morning some two miles distant from Chandá Sáhib's post, and in front of the very strongest part of Law's position. This was an opportunity which any other commander but Law would have seized. He had recognised Dalton's danger, and he had him in his power. But the danger of his own situation had mastered his mental faculties. He allowed Dalton to fall back unmolested; then, against the positive orders of Dupleix, against the entreaties of Chandá Sáhib, despite the remonstrances of all his commanders, he retreated into the island of Srirangam, abandoning or destroying a great part of the provisions accumulated for the use of his European troops.

Then followed a series of catastrophes, the consequences of this false move. A letter from D'Auteuil, intimating his movements, fell into the hands of the English, and Lawrence despatched Clive to intercept D'Auteuil, as he should approach the western bank of the Kolrún. But Chandá Sáhib, well served by spies, communicated to Law the movement of Clive, and pointed out to him the possibility of crushing that leader whilst he was endeavouring to crush D'Auteuil. The manœuvre could scarcely fail, if it were executed in sufficient force, and with sufficient intelligence. Law did recognise in this plan a certain chance of extricating himself from all his troubles. The river Kaverí and its branches would prevent the possibility of any assistance reaching Clive. He might move out with his entire force. No enemy would attempt Srirangam. But again his caution spoilt a plan, the success of which was assured. Instead of marching with his whole force to crush Clive, he despatched only 80 Europeans, of whom 40 were English deserters, and 700 sipáhis. Even this small detachment went very near to success. It surprised Clive whilst he was asleep at Simiáveram, and, but for the extraordinary coolness, audacity, and presence of mind displayed by that great soldier, must have captured or killed him. But the value of one man never asserted itself more convincingly than on the night of that memorable surprise. After braving death in every form Clive emerged from it the victor, and the despondency of Law became greater than ever.

Nor was D'Auteuil more successful. Escorting supplies of ammunition and food, he had reached the Utátur, spoken of in a previous chapter. Dalton, with a force about equal in numbers, had been sent to watch him. As he approached Utátur, Dalton, who was as daring as his enemy was timid, so arranged his troops as to induce the belief that the whole British force was advancing. D'Auteuil fell into the trap, and retreated on Volkonda without striking a blow, leaving to Dalton the stores and ammunition he had escorted.

Soon after this event, the final catastrophe followed. After all his losses, Law could still dispose of 800

Frenchmen, 2000 trained sipáhis, and 3000 or 4000 horsemen who still remained faithful to Chandá Sáhib. With these he could, without much risk, have fought his way to the coast. But the spirit of the man was utterly broken. Whilst those about him were talking of fighting, he was dreaming of surrender. On the 13th of June he carried out this dream, after having vainly stipulated for the life of his ally. The result was that Chandá Sáhib was stabbed to the heart, and that 35 French officers, 785 soldiers, and 2000 trained sipáhis, surrendered themselves as prisoners.

It is time now to note how Dupleix received the news of this terrible calamity, and what steps he took to minimise its effects.

CHAPTER IX

A Great Man Wrestling with Fortune

In the preceding chapter, writing of the attempt made to surprise Clive at Samiáveram, I have used these words: 'The value of one man never asserted itself more convincingly than on the night of that memorable surprise.' *Mutatis mutandis*, the same words might be applied to the conduct of Dupleix when he learned of the shameful surrender of his whole European force, save the detachments under Bussy and D'Auteuil, to Major Lawrence at Srirangam.

The blow was undeniably a very severe blow. It left the English triumphant; their ally, Muhammad Alí, master of the Karnátik; the prestige—that word of enormous importance in India—of the French lowered. But, with the clear-headedness habitual with him, Dupleix, far from despairing, took stock of his actual position. He recognised fully the extent of the catastrophe consummated at Srirangam; and that south of the river Krishtna he could dispose only of the troops under D'Auteuil, insufficient even for garrison purposes. Yet, he had still the Subáhdár of the Deccan at his back. The unbeaten

Bussy was at Aurangábád, holding secure the predominating influence of Pondichery. He held Gingí, then considered the strongest fortress in the Karnátik, and the possessions on the coast secured to France by the Subáhdár. On the other hand, whilst the total force at his disposal was, as I have said, insufficient to supply garrisons to guard these posts, he had in front of him a triumphant enemy, with numerous native allies, commanded by a Lawrence and a Clive. That enemy had it in his power to effect enormous mischief to French interests. It could even destroy that influence. What was he to do?

It was in this conjuncture that the profound knowledge which Dupleix had acquired of the native character stood him in good stead. He knew, from previous observation, that for a number of native chiefs allied to effect a specific purpose the day of triumph was the day of trial. Now, to assist in crushing Chandá Sáhib, Muhammed Alí had called in the levies of Tanjore, of Mysore, and the Maráthás. To work upon the most powerful of these, to sow jealousy between them, to plant distrust of Muhammad Alí, all unable as he would be to fulfil, with an empty exchequer, the lavish promises made in the hour of need, became then the main occupation of the French Governor. No one better than he could accomplish a task beset indeed with difficulties, yet promising to a man experienced in the native modes of thought the most brilliant advantage.

He did not work in vain. When the first triumph

of his victory had evaporated, Muhammad Alí found that the only fruit of his victory was the death of his rival. The troops of Tanjore clamoured to be permitted to return to their homes. The Maráthás refused to serve with the troops of Mysore, and the latter declined to be instrumental in pushing further the interests of Muhammad Alí. The disputes became so hot that both the contingents last-named drew off in a huff, making hostile demonstrations against the English. The discords had meanwhile prevented action, and it was not till the 9th of July that Muhammad Alí and the English were able to quit Trichinopoli. Even then, they were forced to leave in that fortress a garrison of 200 Englishmen and 1500 trained sipáhis to protect it against their former allies.

The delay thus caused had been eminently serviceable to Dupleix. During that month the first portion of the annual drafts from France had arrived. They were few in number, and a very ragged lot, but by replacing the sailors of the vessels by lascars, and enlisting the former, Dupleix was able to dispose of 500 additional men. In another way Fortune came to help him. Major Lawrence and Clive had both been forced by ill-health to proceed to Madras, and the command of the English was left to the not very capable De Gingen. The force was occupying Tiruvádí, a place they had taken from the French, when, contrary to the advice of Lawrence, the English Governor, Saunders, transmitted to De Gingen orders to attack the strong fortress of Gingi. That officer promptly despatched 200 English, 500 trained sipáhis, and 600 of Muhammad Alí's cavalry on this expedition.

This was the opportunity for which Dupleix had been longing. He seized it with the avidity of a great commander. Despatching orders to the commandant of Gingi to hold himself on the alert, he directed his nephew, De Kerjean, to march with 300 of the new levies and 500 sipáhis to occupy a position which, whilst the English were before Gingi, would sever their communications with the coast.

The manœuvre met with the success it deserved. Gingi was a very strong place, and when the English commander, Kinneer, arrived in front of it, he recognised that the task set to him was, for him at least, impossible. Just then information reached him that a French force had occupied a position in his rear which completely cut him off from his supplies and the coast. Kinneer turned to attack this force, but was beaten with the loss of forty of his Englishmen, and with difficulty made his way back to Tiruvádí. About the same time, a French ship captured a vessel having on board a company of Swiss mercenaries on their way to reinforce the English.

Thus, within two months from the surrender of Law, Dupleix had by his energy, his intrigues, and his daring done much to obliterate the English triumph at Trichinopoli and to neutralise its effects. His action in this crisis alone would stamp him as a most eminent servant of his country. The position he held was one exactly suited to the talents with which he had been gifted. When the hopes of France were at their lowest he had organised victory out of the crudest materials, and, in an incredibly brief period, had managed to re-clothe the French name with the prestige which the feebleness of Law had done so much to diminish.

Proofs of this followed upon De Kerjean's successful campaign. He received from the Subáhdár his formal appointment as Nuwáb of the Karnátik; from the Mysore troops and the Maráthás, so recently leagued against him, promises of active co-operation if he would but leave them free to prosecute their views on Trichinopoli. From his sovereign, Louis XV, Dupleix received at this time the patent of the title of Marquis.

All at once it seemed as though the positions of the French and English, so marked at the time of the surrender of Law, had been suddenly reversed. Whilst Dupleix encouraged his native allies to besiege Trichinopoli, he considered himself strong enough to detach a force to blockade Fort St. David. That force, commanded by De Kerjean, consisted of 400 Frenchmen, 1500 sipáhis, and 500 horsemen. But this was too much for the lion-hearted Stringer Lawrence. Rousing himself from his bed of sickness, he came from Madras to Fort St. David, and, with troops equal in number to those of his adversary, forced De Kerjean to fall back to within three miles of

Pondichery. There he dared not attack him, as the territory was French, and as such was secured against attack by treaty. The French were equally bound to inaction by the fact that Dupleix was momentarily expecting the arrival of 700 trained troops under the young and brilliant De la Touche, an arrival which would seemingly place all the possibilities within his grasp. Lawrence knew this, and anxious to strike a blow before the fresh troops should arrive, yet debarred from attacking De Kerjean where he was, used all his efforts to entice his enemy beyond the border-line. With this object he fell back to a place called Báhur, two miles from Fort St. David. De Kerjean, young, ambitious, knowing that any day he might be superseded by De la Touche, followed up his retreating foe, and on the morning of September 6 attacked him. The action was the most fiercely contested of the whole war. The Europeans on both sides fought splendidly. The result was decided by the falling back at a critical moment of the French sipáhis, stationed in the centre of the line. Lawrence pushed on and achieved a complete victory. The English lost eighty-three officers and men killed and wounded. On the French side, De Kerjean himself, fifteen officers, and about 100 men were taken prisoners. Their loss in killed and wounded was never ascertained [1].

[1] Lawrence, and, following Lawrence, Orme, state that, when prisoner, De Kerjean declared that he was forced into action by the repeated orders of Dupleix. There is no proof of this beyond the word of a man anxious to justify himself at the expense of another. On

This was a blow, and what was worse, a blow which a little prudence would have avoided. Its effects were quickly visible in the cooling of the new-born enthusiasm of the Maráthá and Mysore troops. The coolness was not, however, proof against the methods of Dupleix. When the leaders of those troops noted that Lawrence remained inactive after his victory, and took no steps to improve it, they, after a momentary hesitation, openly declared for the French.

Dupleix gained, too, another advantage at this period by the compulsory departure of Clive for Europe. That brilliant chief, after recovering from the fever which had taken him to Madras, had won back for Muhammad Alí nearly the whole of North Arcot, had routed a force sent by Dupleix to relieve Covelong, had taken that place and Chengalpat, the strongest fortress after Gingi in Southern India, and had then proceeded to England. Lawrence, however, still remained, and Lawrence was very decidedly a man to be feared.

Still, if De la Touche and his 700 men would but arrive, there was hope that even Lawrence might be foiled. De la Touche had never been beaten: he had displayed all the qualities which entitle a man to command his fellows—he had no fear of responsibility, was active, daring, and intelligent. From him much was to be hoped. The despair, the agony

the other hand, there is reason to believe that Dupleix was anxious to avoid an action until De la Touche should arrive.

of Dupleix may be imagined, when, instead of De la Touche and his men, information reached him that the ship which was conveying them to India, the *Prince*, had been destroyed by fire with all on board.

This was indeed a blow sufficient to daunt the boldest. During the second half of 1752 Dupleix had improvised resources to make head against the preponderance which the surrender of Law had given to his enemies. He had done this confident that the succeeding year would witness the transference of the preponderance to himself. In that hope he had laboured to detach from the English the most powerful of their native allies, had made soldiers of the crews of the merchant vessels, had drawn largely upon his own private financial resources; and, but for the precipitancy of De Kerjean, would have almost neutralised the effects of the surrender of Srirangam. When the 700 troops under De la Touche should join the 360 still at Pondichery, he would be able to range against the enemy upwards of 1000 men, commanded by a man from whom he was justified in expecting great results. And now, by an accident which he could neither have foreseen nor prevented, he was deprived of these succours which would have given him that superiority. He was to meet the new year with but 360 European troops, whilst the English could put 700 into the field. He was to meet it still without a general, whilst the English had Stringer Lawrence. He was to meet it knowing that he was left by his country to his own resources; that from it no assistance was to be expected. For a man with the soaring aspirations of Dupleix, no position could have seemed more hopeless. But it was the surpassing merit of Dupleix that in the darkest hour he never despaired. Confident in his own energies, in his greater knowledge of the races of Southern India, believing that with but a little aid from Fortune his genius must compensate for the superiority of his enemy in European troops, he prepared himself for the struggle of the new year with an alacrity and a resolution which to this day compels the admiration even of those who rejoice over his failure.

CHAPTER X

Too Heavily Handicapped

Nothing appeals so much to human sympathy as the sight of a great man struggling with adverse Fortune. To see him with a bold and unshaken front defying her frowns, rising superior to disaster, improvising resources; seizing every advantage, improving it to such a degree that even his enemies come to regard his personality alone as the foe to be feared—that is a sight which few can regard unmoved. Such a display was given to the world in 1814 by the greatest warrior of modern times, when he, at bay against combined Europe, almost succeeded in compelling Fortune. The story of that wonderful campaign has provoked sympathy and admiration from nationalities who hated the man. There was a marked resemblance in feature and in genius between Napoleon and Dupleix. Each was animated by unbounded ambition, each played for a great stake; each displayed, in the final struggle, a power and a vitality, a richness of resource and a genius such as compelled fear and admiration: both, alas, were finally abandoned by their countrymen. But their names still remain, and will ever remain, to posterity as examples of the enormous value, in a struggle with adversity, of a dominant mind directed by a resolute will.

Reduced by the accident to the *Prince* to a position which any ordinary man would have regarded as one essentially defensive, Dupleix, feeling about him, set to work to ascertain the mode in which he could best neutralise the enemy's superiority in European soldiers. No more difficult problem could have presented itself to him. Since the victory of Paradis on the Adyár, Europeans had been regarded as the kernel of an army in India. Their superiority, maintained to the present day, was admitted in all the territories south of the Vindhyan Range. Bussy, with a handful of men, was maintaining that superiority at the Court of the Subáhdár. Thanks to the same superiority, the English, at the beginning of 1753, held a marked predominance in the Karnátik. But it might, Dupleix thought, by judicious management be so far neutralised as to procure for him a striking advantage on the decisive point. To this end he applied all his efforts.

Negotiating skilfully, he soon ascertained that he could dispose of the 2000 trained sipáhis and the 4000 Maráthá horse, commanded by a Maráthá chief of great ability as a leader, named Morárí Ráo. As Muhammad Alí could muster but 1500 horsemen, and those inferior in all respects to the Maráthás, Dupleix, by this alliance, was able to possess a marked advantage in cavalry. The Regent of Mysore, too, displayed a readiness not only to furnish troops to aid the French, but to command them in person. Under the circumstances, then, Dupleix hoped that, judiciously employing the resources thus available to him, he might so plan his campaign that his superiority in cavalry and in native troops generally might atone for and neutralise the great superiority of his enemy in Europeans. With this end in view, he resolved, in consultation with his allies, that whilst the Mysore troops should invest Trichinopoli, the French troops and Morárí Ráo should act as in a certain sense a covering army to baffle all the attempts which Lawrence might make to relieve the beleaguered place. They would, in a word, keep Lawrence employed. Having regard to the superiority in cavalry which Dupleix could command, we are bound to admit that no more skilful plan could have been devised. If the league could be maintained, the want of provisions would compel the surrender of Trichinopoli.

At the outset, the plan worked well. Whilst the Mysore army blockaded Trichinopoli, Morárí Ráo and the French contingent, under the command of M. Maissin, took up an intrenched position on the river Punar, near the English post of Tiruvádí, seven miles from Fort St. David. From this post they commenced a series of harassing movements against the English, cutting off their supplies, capturing foraging parties, and rendering it very difficult for the garrison of Tiruvádí to communicate with that of Fort St. David. In vain did Lawrence do his utmost to bring them to action. On his approach, the allies withdrew behind their intrenchments. To such a state of distress was he reduced at last that he found himself compelled to employ his whole force as an escort to convoys whose arrival was necessary for the provision of supplies. It need not be told how service of this nature harassed and distressed his men.

During three months the allies persisted in their policy. More than one opportunity was offered them of inflicting serious damage on the convoys and the troops escorting them, but they were not taken. Lawrence, however, felt so keenly the danger threatening English interests from the existence of an intrenched camp so close to Fort St. David whilst Trichinopoli, invested by the Mysore troops, was crying for relief, that he determined to take advantage of the arrival of 200 Europeans from Madras to storm the intrenchment. But a reconnaissance in force, and the failure of a sharp fire from his two 24-pounders to make any impression on the defences, showed him that the attempt could not succeed. Irritated and anxious, he waited three weeks longer, hoping some chance might offer. Instead of such a chance, he received, at the close of that period, despatches from Dalton, who commanded in Trichinopoli, telling him that he had but three weeks' supplies of provisions, and that he was blockaded on all sides. Lawrence did not hesitate a moment. Leaving 150 Europeans and 500 sipáhis under Captain Chace to defend Tiruvádí, he marched with the remainder of his troops, amounting to 650 Europeans and 1500 sipáhis, for Trichinopoli.

The sudden departure of Lawrence did not escape the watchful eye of Dupleix. Early in the year he had despatched 100 French troops—obtained partly from Bengal, partly from the ships in the roadstead—to co-operate with the soldiers of Mysore, and these men had occupied the island of Srirangam. Confident that the move of Lawrence was directed against Trichinopoli, he despatched on the instant 200 Frenchmen and 500 sipáhis from Maissin's force to reinforce the garrison of Srirangam, leaving in the intrenched position on the Punar 160 Europeans and 1500 sipáhis. The command of the detached force he gave to M. Astruc, an officer who had given signs of capacity. Whilst Astruc is marching on Sriringam, I propose to watch the action of Maissin on the Punar.

Recognising at a glance that Lawrence had staked the fortunes of his countrymen on the successful defence of Trichinopoli, Dupleix determined to avail himself, to the full extent of the resources left to him, of the advantages within his reach. He could not attack Fort St. David, for that place was secured to England by treaty. But Tiruvádí and Chilambaram—a strong post on the road to Trichinopoli—had slender garrisons, whilst the provinces of North and South Arcot were left almost entirely denuded of English troops. These then he could recover. Acting on the powers bestowed upon him by the Subáhdár he had nominated Murtizá Alí, a relation of the deceased Chandá Sáhib, to be Nuwáb of the Karnátik. In his name, whilst Lawrence was chained to Trichinopoli, he would recover that territory. He sent then positive instructions to Maissin to storm Tiruvádí. Maissin attacked (May 3), and was repulsed; attacked again a few days later, and was again driven back. On the second occasion, however, the English garrison, not content with repulsing their enemy, followed him into the field. There they were surrounded by the Maráthá horsemen, and cut to pieces to a man. Tiruvádí then surrendered; Chilambaram followed suit; then Murtizá Alí started with a considerable native force and fifty French soldiers to recover the strong places in North and South Arcot. To a very large extent he succeeded, defeating the supporters of Muhammad Alí in a pitched battle, and clearing the provinces, except in the vicinity of Trichinopoli, of active enemies.

Lawrence, meanwhile, marching rapidly, had entered Trichinopoli the 6th of May. But sickness and desertions had greatly reduced his force. When he mustered his troops after his arrival he found he could put into the field, including the soldiers which the garrison could spare, only 500 Europeans, 80 artillery-men, 2000 sipáhis, and 3000 of rabble cavalry in the service of Muhammad Alí. With this force he marched to drive the French from Srirangam. But the reinforcements despatched by Dupleix had reached that island the day after Lawrence had arrived at Trichinopoli. A reconnaissance in force then convinced Lawrence that the island was too strong to be attempted. Indeed, it was as much as he could do, to use his own language[1], 'by a very brisk fire of artillery, to keep our flanks clear from the cavalry that surrounded us, and at every movement we made were ready to charge. Nor were the enemy's cannon silent.' The consequence was that after a very fatiguing day Lawrence was forced to retreat at night across the river, having lost two officers killed and three wounded, but he states, 'very few men in proportion.' At this period Colonel Lawrence's health failed him, and he withdrew within the fort. His situation there was a difficult one, for he was dependent upon native allies for supplies, and, since the capture of Chilambaram by the French, the road from the coast was in the hands of the enemy. By this time too, Dupleix, by incredible exertions, had so increased the force under Astruc that it slightly out-numbered, in Europeans, the number of which Lawrence could dispose.

Noting all these things, Astruc, who was then very daring, obeying the instructions transmitted from Pondichery, crossed the Káverí, and took possession of a commanding position known as the 'Five Rocks.' This position, if held, must compel the surrender of the fortress, as it commanded the country, known as

[1] *Vide* Cambridge's *War in India*, containing Colonel Lawrence's *Narrative of the War on the Coast of Coromandel*, from the beginning of the troubles to the year 1754, page 59.

the 'Tondeman's country,' whence the English obtained their native supplies.

In another work[1], I have given in full detail the story of the exciting military events which followed. In this work it is necessary only to record the results. My object is to place as clearly as I can before the reader the marvellous recuperative power of Dupleix, the persistently steady aim of his policy, his unswerving confidence in ultimate success, his determination to leave nothing untried to achieve it. Let the reader contrast his position at the beginning of 1753, when the loss of the 700 men coming from France under De la Touche and the death with them of that promising soldier, left him with scanty and inferior numbers to continue the battle for empire against Stringer Lawrence and the English, with the position his genius, his exertions, his ever-active brain had created in June of the same year. It was indeed a triumph of statesmanship. Whilst his troops under Bussy held in the French interest the territories of the Subáhdár, comprehending those now ruled by the Nizam; whilst he had even obtained, by the tact and readiness of Bussy, the cession to France of the country called the 'Northern Sirkars'; he had recovered for the Nuwáb nominated by himself North and South Arcot, had compelled the English to surrender Tiruvádí and Chilambaram, and to hold Fort St. David with a scanty garrison; had once more forced them to act on the defensive at Trichinopoli, and had severed

[1] *History of the French in India.* Longmans, 1866.

their connection with the coast. Nay, more. On that spot, near to which the ill-fated Law had surrendered with nearly 700 Europeans only one year before, Dupleix had so managed as to bring the greater number to bear against the lesser. The difference indeed was but trifling, but to accomplish it at all, in the face of the initial disaster of the year, was a marvellous achievement. He had done everything, in fact, that a comprehensive human brain could do. By the force of that brain alone he had inverted the position of the two nations in Southern India. In June, 1752, Law and the entire French army surrendered at Sriringam. In June, 1753, Astruc occupied a position in front of Trichinopoli, whilst the English were content to defend the place. There is but one way of accounting for such a startling inversion of position. His supplies from Europe had failed him, whilst the English had received theirs. Driven to depend upon himself alone, Dupleix had, by a combination carried through without a check, so far compelled Fortune that it seemed to require but a great effort on the part of his army to win her over completely.

It was supremely unfortunate for him, specially fortunate for his rivals, that in Stringer Lawrence the English possessed one of the most capable men who ever served the East India Company. He was a great soldier; and his modesty equalled his daring. It is impossible to read his narrative of the war without being struck by the noble and unselfish nature of the man, by his great talent as a commander, by his coolness and readiness of resource on all occasions. He had a most able assistant in Captain Dalton, whose Memoirs, published a few years ago, throw much light on the splendid spirit which animated our countrymen fighting in a strange country and with half-hearted allies. There was scarcely a man amongst them who was not a hero, and it is well that their memory, the memory of men who laid, in Southern India, the foundation of the wider Empire held by their descendants, should remain green and fresh for all time. For, after all, it was Clive, and Lawrence, and Dalton, and their companions, who foiled Dupleix. Had they not been better than the French officers to whom they were opposed, Dupleix must have won the game. He was their superior in his knowledge of native character, in his influence over the natives, in his powers of combination. But he was not a soldier. He could plan a campaign; could direct his lieutenants what to do. But he could not act amid the storm of bullets and the roar of cannon. In that respect Clive and Lawrence surpassed not only him, but the lieutenants whom he sent to carry out his instructions. It was this superiority in the field that foiled him. It had made Law surrender in 1752. It completely baffled Astruc and his successors in 1753.

For, pitted against Astruc, Lawrence proved conclusively his superiority. By a sudden manœuvre, Astruc had seized the Golden Rock, expelling thence the English. If he could but hold it, the English were doomed. Lawrence recognised this fact on the moment. Instantly he acted. Suddenly with his whole force he smote the French in front and on their flank, and drove them headlong from the Rock, capturing two guns and calmly defying all the efforts of the Maráthá cavalry to break his square as it retired. To Astruc the defeat was so mortifying that he resigned his command, and returned to Pondichery. He was succeeded by M. Brennier.

Brennier had no better fortune. Lawrence having moved eastward to escort into the fort provisions of which the garrison was in great need, Brennier thought the opportunity good to attempt to storm the place. As a preliminary, he sent into it disguised a Frenchman named De Cattans to sketch the defences. De Cattans was caught in the act by Dalton. Dalton promised to intercede with Lawrence for his life, provided he would indicate to Brennier such points of attack as Dalton should point out. This was done. The stratagem, however, came to nothing, as when the paper reached Brennier he was occupied with another plan, that of intercepting and destroying Lawrence and his convoy.

But in this he was foiled. From the summit of the Trichinopoli Rock, which rises to the height of 1878 feet above the plain, Dalton was able to signal to Lawrence the positions occupied by the French. The consequence was that in the battle which followed, and which was most severely contested, Brennier was completely defeated. Totally demoralised, he fled to the banks of the Káverí. Here, to his surprise, he was joined by Astruc, bringing reinforcements of 400 Europeans, six guns, 2000 sipáhis, and 3000 Maráthá horse. Astruc took the command.

Astruc was a more capable man than Brennier, and he had now a great opportunity, for his total of Europeans exceeded that of Lawrence, whilst his horsemen surpassed those of Muhammad Alí alike in quality as well as in number. It was indeed hard on Dupleix, to whose splendid exertions the despatch of this reinforcement was due, that at such a conjuncture Astruc should have become over-cautious. The third day after his arrival he had enticed the English force into a position in which it could be assailed with advantage. The Maráthá chief, Morárí Ráo, pointed out to Astruc the opportunity, and implored him to use it, but afraid to risk all on the issue of a battle, Astruc declined. He had reason to repent it, for a fortnight later Lawrence received a reinforcement of 237 Europeans, under a very able soldier, Captain Calliaud. Four days after the arrival of this reinforcement, 1st October, 1753, Lawrence marched out and offered battle to Astruc. Astruc declined it. Thereupon Lawrence encamped where he stood, attacked him the following morning, and completely defeated him, taking prisoners Astruc himself, nine officers, and ninety-one men, capturing eleven guns, and killing or wounding about 100 men. His own loss did not exceed twenty men and six officers killed and wounded. The rest of the French force found refuge in the island of Srirangam.

Meanwhile Dupleix at Pondichery, whilst using all the means in his power to strengthen his force before Trichinopoli, had not been less persistent in his attempts to pacify the Karnátik. More than one circumstance, slight in itself, had satisfied him that his masters in France were men who would judge only by results; that whilst they were ready to applaud and flatter him so long as he was successful, they would unhesitatingly sacrifice him if Fortune should prove adverse. Success, to them, meant the peaceful acquisition of territory, and increase of trading facilities. They cared not to reason out the terms by which such success was to be acquired. Why Dupleix should send troops to be killed before Trichinopoli was a problem they declined to consider. They only saw the result; that, so far as concerned Trichinopoli, failure had succeeded failure. In the bosom of the French Company there had always been a minority jealous of Dupleix, feeble at first in its action, but always ready to start into active life. It was at this period, that is, after the surrender of Law had become known, that this minority began to assert its existence. In spite of its efforts, the majority had despatched De la Touche and his 700 men to reinforce Dupleix. The accident which had disposed of this strong force before it reached the shores of India, whilst it deprived Dupleix of a strength which, considering all that he effected without it, he would probably have made decisive, served, illogically yet most certainly, to strengthen the enemies of the great proconsul. When, after the information reached France that Dupleix was still fighting, wasting, as it was argued, in military expeditions resources which should have been carefully utilised to develop commercial enterprise, the shareholders became dissatisfied, and the minority in the Council of Directors became formidable. Despatches were sent out to him, in which the necessity of procuring peace at any price was insisted upon in language not to be misunderstood.

Dupleix was not unwilling to have peace. He would himself indeed have preferred to be at peace with the English, provided only that they would recognise the titles and the concessions he had obtained from the Subáhdár of the Deccan. These concessions included (December, 1753) the whole of the territory known as the Northern Sirkars. He had already, in February of 1792, addressed Mr. Saunders on the subject; but the reply he received plainly showed him that the English would not then admit his pretensions. When, however, in July of 1753, he had the first glimmering of the possible attitude towards himself of his masters in France, he attempted to renew the negotiation. The time, the reader will recollect, was when Lawrence and Astruc faced one another, not unequally, before Trichinopli; when Dupleix was recovering North and South Arcot; when Moracin, sent for the purpose by Bussy, was organising the territories of the Chilka Lake and Motapili. The reply of Saunders was conciliatory, and negotiations opened. It soon transpired, however, that the French demands were of a nature which the English Governor would never concede. Dupleix demanded, as a preliminary, the recognition by the English of himself as Nuwáb of the Karnátik. To admit this demand, Saunders felt, was to grant all that the two nations had been fighting for. In vain did Dupleix urge that the title had been bestowed by the Subáhdár of the Deccan, and confirmed by a farmán from the Mughal Emperor. Saunders replied that the title had descended to Muhammad Alí, as the surviving son of his father, and that he would not renounce it. The negotiations, however, continued. But it soon became clear that the issue of them would depend upon the result of the military proceedings before Trichinopoli. Should Astruc succeed in beating Lawrence, why, then the question would resolve itself. Each of the negotiating parties felt this. Each, therefore, whilst negotiating, strained every nerve to strengthen his forces before the rock-fortress.

To Mr. Saunders, and the English generally, it seemed that that question had been fully decided on the 2nd of October. The loss to the French of 200 Europeans, the capture of their leader, and the retreat of the remainder of the force into Srirangam, seemed a blow from which it would be impossible to recover. That Lawrence thought so is clear from the fact that instead of pursuing the dispirited remnants of the

French force into Srirangam, he had, after taking Waikonda, cantoned his army at Koiládí, fifteen miles to the east of Trichinopoli, commanding the approaches from the coast to the island. But Dupleix was not the man to give in whilst a chance remained. Never was he more formidable than when he had been apparently crushed. Never, I may add, did he show himself greater than on this occasion. According to all rule he was crushed. His best army had been defeated, his best general taken prisoner, the disheartened remnant of his soldiers were crouching in Srirangam—place of fatal omen—and Lawrence, with his victorious army, seemed to bar the way from Pondichery. But Dupleix did not give up the game. He had recently received from France reinforcements sufficient to enable him to dispose of 300 Europeans. Joining to these 1200 sipáhis, he despatched them under the orders of a new commander, De Mainville[1], with definite instructions. These were to join as secretly as possible the force in Srirangam, to lull the English into security; then, suddenly emerging from the island, to carry Trichinopoli by a *coup de main*.

The report that the English force was suffering greatly from sickness at Koiládí had reached Dupleix. It was very true. In a few days Lawrence had lost six officers and many men. He had dismissed to

[1] Lawrence, and after him Orme, state that Maissin commanded: but the French records show that it was Mainville, and that the command was not given to Maissin until after the arrival of Godeheu to relieve Dupleix.

their own country the Tanjore troops, and he was supported only by the rabble of Muhammad Alí. It was under these circumstances that Mainville marched. He reached the island in safety, and remained there so quiet that Lawrence, busy with his sick troops, conceived no suspicion as to his intentions. All this time Mainville was making preparations, preparing scaling ladders, training his men, and storing up information about the fortress. At length, on December 8, he was ready. He had acted with so much caution that neither the English nor their native allies entertained the slightest suspicions as to his intentions. His plan was as follows: To attempt with 600 Frenchmen, supported by 200 more and the sipáhis, the part of the rock-fortress known as Dalton's Battery, guarded, it had been ascertained, by only fifty sipáhis; after mastering this, without firing a shot, to dash round the two traverses, guided by a deserter, and apply a petard to the gate of the town: should that fail, to attempt to escalade, the walls at that point being but eighteen feet above the rock.

At three o'clock in the morning of December 9 (new style), Mainville crossed the Káverí to carry out his plan; reached, unperceived, the base of the rock; and stormed Dalton's Battery without losing a man. Had his men only obeyed orders and abstained from firing, they would certainly have captured the place, for the English were fast asleep. But the evil genius of the French soldiers prompted them to turn against the town two of the twelve-pounders they had captured in Dalton's Battery, and to shout *Vive le Roi*. The result was to arouse the garrison. To such purpose indeed did the noise rouse them, that when the French, guided by the English deserter, dashed round the traverses, they were met by a heavy musketry fire from the hurriedly-assembled garrison. The first fire killed the deserter, the only one of the party who knew the exact locality of the town gate. His death caused delay whilst men were searching for the gate, and meanwhile the English fire became more and more deadly. It was dark, and the numbers on both sides could not be seen. But the English knew perfectly where they were, whilst the French were at a great disadvantage from want of that knowledge. It was not, however, until their ladders had been shattered that they thought of retreating. But they were in an *impasse*. There was no means of escape open to them except by leaping from the battery. This some few attempted, but, when the day broke, the majority, noting that they were quite at the mercy of their enemies, asked for quarter. This was granted to them. 'They lost in this affair,' wrote Lawrence, '364 Europeans taken prisoners, 65 of whom were wounded; 8 officers also taken, most of them wounded, and 1 officer killed, and they acknowledged themselves that many more were wounded or lamed who were carried off to the island.' Lawrence adds: 'The scheme was well laid, and had not French petulance made them too soon discover themselves, they perhaps might have had time to execute their designs.' About this, we think, there can be no reasonable doubt.

This time the blow was fatal: it did not, indeed, come alone. The Nuwáb nominated by Dupleix to rule the Karnátik, Murtizá Alí, had been beaten at Tiruvannámalai, and another French partisan, Muhammad Kumar, had been annihilated before the pagoda of Tirupatí. But the defeat before Trichinopoli was the fatal blow. It was the finishing stroke which paralysed the French Governor. The one chance of recouping himself lay in a prompt accommodation with the English. Could he persuade Saunders to agree to terms of a settlement, no matter how disadvantageous, he might secure at least a respite. It was the more necessary that such a result should follow, as the news from France pointed to the possibility of his being made the scape-goat for all the mishaps. Dupleix found Saunders not unwilling to respond. After a tedious correspondence, it was finally resolved between them that Commissioners from both parties should hold a Congress at Sadras, a Dutch settlement between Madras and Pondichery. In accordance with this agreement Messrs. Palk and Vansittart proceeded to that place on the part of the English to meet there Father Lavaur, M. de Kerjean, and M. Bausset, nominated by Dupleix. The French Commissioners reached Sadras the 21st of January, 1754, and the Congress commenced work the following day.

CHAPTER XI

THE FALL OF DUPLEIX

DUPLEIX, whilst determined to maintain his position as Nuwáb of the Karnátik, had authorised his Commissioners to make such liberal concessions on other points as might, he hoped, induce the English to give way in that one particular. At the first meeting of the Congress, then, they proposed that the arrears due by the English Company on account of the rent for Madras should be remitted, and that thenceforth Madras should become the absolute property of the English; that the expenses they had been put to on account of the war should be defrayed from the revenues of the Karnátik; that the French Company should give to the English Company the necessary securities for freedom of commerce. They proposed to compensate Muhammad Alí by the bestowal upon him of a Government in another part of the Deccan guaranteed to him by the French and English jointly; and to assure to the Rájá of Tanjore, under a similar guarantee, the possession of his territories. They demanded also the evacuation by the English of the fortified places in the interior, with the exception of Punamullu, fifteen miles from Madras, which, with its dependent territories, should become absolutely their own; and the release of the prisoners taken on both sides.

In these proposals, it will be observed, though there was no actual mention of the title of Nuwáb of the Karnátik, it was taken for granted throughout that that title, bestowed by the Subáhdár of the Deccan, and confirmed by the Mughal sovereign, should remain with Dupleix. To this the English Commissioners took objection. They urged that although the patent of the Subáhdár might pass, the confirming letter from Delhí was unsigned[1], and was wanting in the seal of the Prime Minister. They were prepared to give way on many points, but regarding the rights of Muhammad Alí they were inflexible.

It was on this point that the negotiations broke off. Dupleix would not give way. In vain did Saunders instruct his Commissioners to make the most liberal concessions to ensure agreement. He went so far as to offer to declare the office of Nuwáb vacant, on condition that Muhammed Alí should be appointed to it under the joint protection of the two Companies. But the passions of Dupleix were roused. He had been formally nominated Nuwáb of the Karnátik. His pride would not allow him to renounce so lofty a position in favour of a man who had posed as his rival. Seventy years later, the man whom he most resembled in ambition, in genius, in the power of compelling others, came, under similar

[1] My own experience points to the fact that native sovereigns rarely affix their signatures to documents of this description.

circumstances, at Dresden in 1813, and at Chatillon in 1814, to a similar resolution. He, too—to use the words of the English historian—'refused to sit on a degraded throne.' It was the one occasion throughout that long war on which Dupleix allowed his passions to master his reasoning powers. What if he had given way? Men of that stamp give way only to make a further step forward. Had he agreed to forego his own pretensions and to acknowledge Muhammad Alí, not only would he have received back all his soldiers, but an opportunity would have been granted him to employ his unrivalled powers of intrigue upon his whilom enemy. Who, that knows Asiatics, can doubt his success? It was certain that, sooner or later, and rather sooner than later, the relations between Muhammad Alí and the English, the obliged and the obliger, would become strained. Then, could he but remain quiet up to that time, nursing his resources, his chance would come. And it would have been a great chance. Some thought of this sort, doubtless, occurred to Dupleix. But his pride rejected it; and his pride went before his fall.

In consequence of the failure of the negotiations at Sadras, hostilities before Trichinopoli were renewed. Strange to relate, the first actions seemed to justify the obstinacy of Dupleix at the Congress. He, too, had his battle of Dresden. Acting in concert with Morárí Ráo, Mainville laid an ambush in force for a large convoy, escorted by the famous grenadiers who had borne the brunt of the battles of Lawrence, 184 in number, 800 sipáhis, and four guns. The French blocked the road with 240 European infantry[1], 6000 sipáhis, and a troop of 80 European horsemen, near Kantapára, seven miles from Trichinopoli, whilst Morárí Ráo, with 3500 native horsemen, lay in ambush in some thick woods. The surprise was complete (February 26); the English in long single file could offer no efficient resistance. They could only die at their posts. The horsemen had already killed fifty of them when the French infantry came up. They at once offered quarter. The offer was accepted, and 134 Englishmen, of whom 100 were wounded, became prisoners to the French. Of the English officers, four were killed, three were taken prisoners, and one escaped. The victors captured likewise four pieces of cannon, about £7000 in money, and the convoy of provisions.

But this success was only a flash in the pan. On the 23rd of May a force of 700 Frenchmen, supported by a large body of sipáhis and Maráthá horse, was repulsed by an English force much inferior in numbers. It was an occasion which, had the French been well led, might have proved decisive of the war; for, for some time, the English were in great peril. But the resources of Dupléix were by no means exhausted. Under his orders Mainville, by a skilful

[1] Lawrence says, '120 French infantry, two companies of deserters about the same number, the French troop of about eighty, 6000 sipáhis, all the Mysore cavalry and the Maráthás, in all about 10,000 and seven pieces of cannon.'

movement, possessed himself of Kilakota and Koiládí, whilst Morárí Ráo defeated the Tanjore troops. Bringing his diplomacy to bear at the opportune moment, Dupleix had almost succeeded in detaching the Rájá of Tanjore from the English alliance when he learned that he had been superseded, and that his successor, M. Godeheu, whom he had formerly benefited at Chandarnagar, and who had subsequently become a Director of the French Company, might arrive at any moment. In fact, the ship carrying Godeheu and his fortunes anchored in the Pondichery roadstead the 1st of August (1754).

The fact was that, in France, the Company of the Indies and the Ministers of the King had alike been long weary of this distant war which brought them neither glory nor profit, but which interfered greatly with commerce. They did not enter into, they did not comprehend, the vastness of the plans of Dupleix, His mind had penetrated the future: their minds were intent on the present. That present had for them a gloomy aspect. As year after year brought no practical result, the idea stole upon them that the resources of France were being squandered to promote the vanity and the ambition of one individual. They reckoned not the advantages already acquired —the control of the councils of the Subáhdár of the Deccan, the most powerful ruler in Southern India; the cession to France in absolute gift of the Northern Sirkars, comprising Gánjám, Vizagapatam, Godávarí. and Krishná, with Rajamahendri and Masulipatam;

the acquisition of important territories round and near to Pondichery; the vast influence exercised by the genius of one man. They were traders, they argued, not soldiers fighting for dominion. They wanted to share peaceably with the English the commerce between Southern India and Europe, not to exterminate rival traders. It is possible that had the policy of Dupleix been immediately successful, the minds of the Directors would have widened so far as to accept results. But when they heard, first of Law's disaster, then of the loss of De la Touche and his 700 men, then of the defeats in succession of Astruc, of Brennier, of Mainville, and found that these military operations interfered greatly with the progress of those commercial relations which they regarded as the reason of their existence, they came at last to the determination to insist on a change of policy. Negotiating with the English East India Company, the Directors of which attributed all the disturbances to Dupleix, they came to the conclusion that that change could be accomplished only if their agent were removed. By them he was considered as the sole obstacle to peace. They resolved then to replace him, to come to terms with their rivals in trade. In vain was it asserted that if Dupleix was responsible for the war, Saunders was not less so. The answer was considered conclusive, that the bellicose humour of Saunders was the necessary consequence of the initiative of Dupleix. There need be but one scape-goat, and it was finally agreed that that scape-goat must be Dupleix. Therefore Godeheu was sent to supersede him.

The ship, the *Duc de Burgogne*, having Godeheu on board, anchored, as I have said, the 1st of August, off Pondichery. Arguing from the previous relations between them, in which he had been the benefactor and Godeheu the benefited, Dupleix went at once on board to welcome his ancient comrade. His reception was most frigid. Godeheu declined to become his guest, or even to land until a house should be fitted up for him. He handed to him, however, three documents: the first a letter expressive of his desire to make his position as little painful as possible; the second a demand for a complete statement of the affairs of the Company; the third an order for his recall. The next day he landed; and, proceeding to the Council Chamber, caused his commission to be read out. The silence which followed the reading was broken by Dupleix, not by the utterance of any querulous complaints, but by the loyal cry *Vive le Roi*.

For ten weeks Dupleix was forced to remain at Pondichery whilst his accounts were overhauled by his successor. Dupleix had advanced to the Company vast sums, and the accounts showed him to be a creditor of the Company to the extent of upwards of £240,000. Godeheu, whose object it seemed to be not merely to belittle but to ruin his predecessor, had no sooner ascertained this fact than he forbad the Commissaries he had employed to proceed further with the accounts, but directed them to give a certificate to the effect that the vouchers produced by Dupleix had reference to the public service. He thus avoided placing on record an acknowledgment of the sums due to Dupleix. But this was not all. Dupleix had been in the habit of advancing large sums from his own private resources to the native allies of France. These advances had been made on the security of certain districts, from the revenues of which they were repayable. At the time of Godeheu's arrival some of the moneys so advanced had been repaid, others, to a very large amount, were still standing over. At the rate however at which the repayments were coming in, the lender would be reimbursed during the following year. But Godeheu, bent on ruining Dupleix, imprisoned the native agent who held the original documents, and declared that the advances had been made by his predecessor for his own private advantage, and not for the benefit of the State. He refused also to allow a bill drawn by the Company in favour of Dupleix to be cashed at Pondichery. Having thus effectually ruined the man who had all but won an Empire for France he allowed him to depart, beggared but not dishonoured, blasted in fortune, cheated out of the fruits of his then ripening labours.

'England,' wrote M. Xavier Raymond in his admirable work on India[1], 'has been much admired and often cited for having resolved the great problem of

[1] *L'Univers Pittoresque*, vol. ii, L'Inde. Paris, 1853.

how to govern, at a distance of 4000 leagues, with some hundreds of civil functionaries and some thousands of soldiers, her immense possessions in India. If there is much that is wonderful, much that is bold and daring, much political genius in the idea, it must be admitted that the honour of having inaugurated it belongs to Dupleix; and that England, which in the present day reaps from it the profit and the glory, has had but to follow the path which the Genius of France opened out to her.' Yes, indeed! Now that the lapse of nearly a century and a half has cleared away the passions and prejudices of that exciting period: now that from the basis of accomplished facts we can examine the ideas and conceptions of the men who were the pioneers of European conquest on Indian soil, there lives not a candid Englishman who will deny to Dupleix the credit of having been the first to devise the method by which European predominance on Indian soil might be established. His work did not endure because it was his misfortune to be compelled to employ inferior tools, whilst his rivals were led by men of extraordinary capacity. It did not last because just at the moment when his plans might have been realised he was recalled at the instance of the immemorial enemy of France, on the eve, moreover, of a war, which for the seven years that were to follow, was to try the resources against France of that very enemy. But the effect of his schemes survived him. The ground he had so well watered and fertilised, the capabilities of which he had proved, was almost immediately after his departure occupied by his rivals, with the immense result which is one of the wonders of the present day.

A body of 2000 French troops had followed Godeheu to India, and had arrived at Pondichery a few days after he had installed himself there as Governor. When we reflect on the great things accomplished by Dupleix with a few hundreds, it is difficult to resist the conclusion that for the interests of France the one superfluous man of all the arrivals was Godeheu himself. Had there been no such arrival, no supersession of Dupleix, these men, in the absence of Clive in England, and of Lawrence, whose health was breaking, would have been sufficient to restore superiority to the French. The outbreak of the war in 1756 between France and England might even have prompted the attack, which Lally subsequently made, upon Madras itself.

It is just possible that this might have been, had the departure of Dupleix from Pondichery been delayed a few weeks longer. A fortnight after he had quitted the shores of India there arrived at that town a despatch from the Controller of Finances in France, M. de Machault, addressed to Dupleix, in which that administrator was referred to as Governor, whilst Godeheu was styled simply the Commissary of the Company, whose sole mission was to treat for peace. There is reason to believe that Machault, an honest man in a corrupt Court, had, very soon after the departure of Godeheu, entertained fears as to the effect of a recall of Dupleix upon French interests in Southern India, and had employed all his address to retain him there as Governor by limiting the responsibilities of Godeheu. He was just too late. His despatch reached Pondichery at the end of October. Dupleix had sailed for Europe on the 14th of that month. The news of his recall had meanwhile spread terror and dismay in those places which he and his subordinates had won for France. Nor were the apprehensions thus caused lessened by the instructions despatched by Godeheu to the French agents in different parts of India to the effect that it was not his intention to interfere in the affairs of native princes. He did not indeed proceed so far as to recall Bussy from Aurangabad, or Moracin from the Northern Sirkars. But both these men felt the difficulties of their position under the new Governor to be so great that it required the most urgent entreaties of Dupleix to persuade them to remain. The reply of Bussy to the entreaty made to himself marks, perhaps as strongly as any other incident, the large principles upon which Dupleix had administered his office, the attachment he had won from those who carried out his behests. 'I reply,' wrote Bussy, 'to the letter with which you favoured me on the 4th. Your departure to Europe is a thunderbolt which has confounded and alarmed me. You, who are leaving, exhort me to continue to serve the nation and to support a work which is on the brink of destruction.

Do you sincerely believe I shall not be enveloped in the same disgrace as yourself? The blow is perhaps deferred, or suspended only to be struck with greater force. But however that may be, I have ever considered it my duty to defer to your counsels and to follow your reasoning. Under no circumstances shall I ever depart from that respectful and inviolable attachment which has been till now my happiness and my glory, and which will always remain so. I await the replies of M. Godeheu before I decide .... If, in the post which I occupy, I am not to be allowed liberty of action; if any attempt be made to fetter me with the ideas of ignorant and inexperienced men, my work must perish in my hands.' Bussy concluded by saying that whilst personally he would prefer to retire to France, he would follow implicitly the advice given him by the man he admired and respected above all others. Dupleix again urgently pressed him to remain, and he remained.

Before I proceed to recount the work of demolition accomplished by Godeheu, and the two subsequent attempts to rebuild on the foundations which Dupleix had laid, I think it due to my readers to accompany that illustrious man in his return to France. His arrival there, strange as it may appear, was looked upon even by some of the men who had recalled him as a misfortune, and for a time it seemed not impossible that he might be directed to return to Pondichery. He was, therefore, well received, and promised a speedy settlement of his claims. But letters from

Godeheu, and the news that he had concluded peace with the English on the spot, at once changed the attitude of the men who ruled. He became then in their eyes an importunate solicitor for the settlement of claims, the payment of which would constitute a heavy tax on their resources. The report of Godeheu, that the claims had not been established to his satisfaction, strengthened their hands. They therefore declined to admit them, or to compensate him in any way. In vain did he remonstrate. In vain did he point out that he was persecuted by creditors who were creditors only, because, on his personal security, they had advanced sums to the State. For seven years he pressed his claims, supporting them by incontestable proofs.

He received not the shadow of redress. Nay, more. Men whom he had befriended, whose fortunes he had made, fell off from him when they saw that he was abandoned by the Government he had served so truly. The state of misery to which he was at last reduced can be realised by the perusal of the following record he made in his Memoirs three days before he died: 'I have sacrificed,' he wrote, 'my youth, my fortune, my life, to enrich my nation in Asia. Unfortunate friends, too weak relations, devoted all their property to the success of my projects. They are now in misery and want. I have complied with all the judiciary forms: I have demanded, as the last of the creditors, that which is due to me. My services are treated as fables, my demand is denounced as ridiculous, I am treated as the vilest of mankind. I am in the most deplorable indigence. The little property that remained to me has been seized. I am compelled to ask for decrees for delay in order not to be dragged to prison.'

Thus wrote, three days before he died, the man who had dug for France the foundations of an Empire which would, if built upon, have made her the arbiter of the East. Nations have their moods of infatuation. In 1754–6 France had hers. Acting in concert with the rival who was to supplant her, she recalled her far-seeing architect, left the foundations desolate and unguarded, and only realised her mistake when she witnessed her rival eagerly adopting those very plans, and building upon those very foundations which the genius of her own architect had devised and marked out. Meanwhile, she had allowed that architect to die 'in misery and want.'

Dupleix died November 10, 1764. Notwithstanding the neglect of his contemporaries, he will ever be regarded as one of the greatest of Frenchmen. Even the rivals who profited by his recall place him on a pedestal scarcely, if at all, lower than the pedestals upon which stand Clive, Warren Hastings, and Wellesley. In grandness of conception, and in the wide scope of his projects of empire, he was their forerunner—unconsciously on their part perhaps, their inspirer.

CHAPTER XII

THE FINAL COLLAPSE

DUPLEIX had departed, and Godeheu reigned in his stead. Godeheu was the exact opposite of his predecessor. He was a man with a mission. That mission was to conclude peace with the English and the native princes at any price. He carried out his task very much to the satisfaction of the English. Only a few months before the English Governor, Saunders, had been ready to conclude a treaty with Dupleix on the principle of admitting all the conditions proposed by the French administrator, if only he would renounce the title of Nuwáb of the Karnátik. Godeheu, who made no pretension to such a title, was glad to assent to terms far less favourable. Thinking only of commerce, and believing that the same sentiment animated the English, he agreed with Saunders that the two Companies should renounce for ever all Mughal dignities and governments, and never interfere in the differences which might arise between the native princes. The second article of his treaty stipulated that whilst the English should possess Madras, Fort St. David, and Devikota, the French should be content with Pondichery, Karikál, and certain districts to be agreed upon, sufficient to make the districts of Pondichery equal to those of Madras and Fort St. David united. On the other hand, the exclusive right of the French to the Northern Sirkars, granted by the Subáhdár, was not recognised. The other conditions related to the navigation of certain rivers, and provided that the principle *uti possidetis* should be applied until the confirmation of the treaty should arrive from Europe. Pending that arrival, no forts were to be erected on either side.

It will be recognised that in this treaty Godeheu renounced all that Dupleix had fought for. He gave up the office of Nuwáb of the Karnátik, he gave up the Northern Sirkars, he gave up his native allies, he gave up the influence and prestige of the French nation. How unfortunate was his administration to France was proved by the fact that whereas to Dupleix, Saunders had offered to yield every point but one—that referring to the Nuwábship of the Karnátik—he reduced Godeheu to a position which left Pondichery and Karikál mere trading-ports. It would seem that his single object was to undo all that Dupleix had accomplished, to renounce all moral influence over the native populations, to abjure the principle of associating for the advantage of France with powerful native sovereigns in the interior. He carried out that programme to the best of his small ability. Only one thing he did not do. He did not recall Bussy and his troops from the Court of the Subáhdár.

Godeheu stayed but a few months in India. He

quitted Pondichery in February, 1755, and was succeeded, after a short interval, by M. Duval de Leyrit, a factor in the employment of the French Company, possessing neither political ability nor large views. He too was a partisan of that policy of non-intervention. He had not been long in office when, May 1756, war broke out between France and England. By this time the French Ministers had realised the enormous mistake they had committed in not efficiently supporting Dupleix, and they notified to De Leyrit that they were preparing a considerable force to send to India to support French interests there. Their original design went far beyond the defence of French interests. The force was to be large enough to expel the English from Southern India, to restore by means of their troops the policy of the Governor they had recalled and ruined.

The command of this expedition was bestowed upon one of the most distinguished officers in the French army, an Irishman by birth. This was Thomas Arthur, Count Lally and Baron Tollendal, son of Sir Gerard O'Lally, who, after the capture of Limerick in 1691, had migrated to France and had entered the service of Louis XIV. Nine years after this event there was born to Sir Gerard the son who, trained from his earliest youth in the French armies, had merited at Fontenoy the commendations of Marshal Saxe; who had taken part in the '45, and had fought at Laffeldt. The young Lally had made a great reputation. His contemporaries regarded him as a man with respect to whom 'it needed only that success should be possible for him to succeed.' The illustrious Voltaire, who had, by desire of the Minister, worked with him a month, recorded that he 'had found in him a stubborn fierceness of soul, accompanied by great gentleness of manners.' In fact, he was universally regarded in France as the man who could take up the dropped thread of the work of Dupleix, and carry it to a successful issue.

It had been originally intended that Lally should sail for India immediately, with a force of 3000 men. The number he actually took fell somewhat short of that total, and what was worse, the delays, caused to a great extent by the incompetence of the Admiral who commanded the fleet which was to co-operate with him, so influenced his proceedings that it was the 28th of April, 1758, before he arrived off Pondichery.

Meanwhile, the treaty concluded between the French and English by Godeheu and Saunders had long since become a dead letter. De Leyrit, noticing the continued infraction of that treaty by his rivals, had been compelled, much against his will, to resume the policy of Dupleix. Rousing the gouty old D'Auteuil from his lethargy, he had despatched him with a superior force to surprise the English at Trichinopoli. D'Auteuil acted as a gouty invalid will always act. Wanting energy, fire, and the sense of the value of prompt action, he, with the most brilliant opportunities before him, allowed himself to be out-manœuvred and beaten back to Pondichery. De Leyrit had then replaced D'Auteuil by one Saubinet, who had done much better, and had compelled the English to act on the defensive. Saubinet was master of the field when the first detachment of Lally's force arrived under the Chevalier de Soupire, (September 9, 1757). Pending the arrival of Lally, De Leyrit united the considerable force of De Soupire to that of Saubinet, and the combined troops captured Tiruvannámalai and other places in the vicinity of Chitapet and Gingi. The opportunities were magnificent to accomplish a great deal more, for the English had sent all the troops they could spare to assist Clive in Bengal. But Lally was expected every day: he was known to be haughty, imperious, violently prejudiced against Franco-Indians. De Soupire hesitated to act decisively till he should arrive: the precious moments, therefore, were allowed to slip by.

At length Lally arrived. He had all the possibilities before him. He was a splendid soldier. But there was wanting, from his disposition, that peculiar quality which had enabled Dupleix to acquire commanding influence over all the native princes with whom he came in contact. Dupleix could persuade: Lally could only command. The one caressed the foibles of the native to turn them to his own advantage. The other heeded neither his foibles nor his virtues, but stamped contemptuously on both. Dupleix, wielding but a small number of European troops, had made possible French predominance in Southern

India because he possessed the innate power of influencing vast numbers of the children of the soil. Lally, wielding a force which, prudently directed, might easily have established that predominance, failed even more miserably than his predecessor for the want of that very tact and knowledge. Not only would he take no pains to conciliate the natives, but he trod ruthlessly on their prejudices. He would recognise none of their castes, and he scoffed openly at their creeds. Nor did he spare the French officials at Pondichery. He treated them with a *hauteur* which soon turned their hearts against him.

It must be admitted, as far as relates to those officials, that they were inefficient and incompetent. Immediately on his arrival, Lally demanded information regarding the strength and garrisons of Fort St. David, of Gudalur, and of Madras; also regarding the total strength of the English in Southern India. But neither De Leyrit nor his councillors could give him any precise information on these points; they could not even tell him the actual distance from Pondichery to Gudalur, though it was but sixteen miles. They could only offer to furnish guides. It is not surprising that this ignorance and this indifference confirmed the contempt of Lally for the Franco-Indian fraternity, nor that thenceforth he utterly disregarded them.

Essentially a man of action, and possessing a superiority in numbers on the coast, Lally obtained at first some striking successes. He took without difficulty both Gudalur and Fort St. David. He then wished to march on Madras. But he had no money; the magazines and arsenals were empty. Instead of a Dupleix to supply the one and fill the other, he had a De Leyrit, who met all his requisitions by pleading the impossibility of complying with them. Strange reversal of position! From 1752 to 1756 Dupleix had improvised the most ample resources for an army: he only wanted the army and the general. In 1758 the army and the general were there, but the incapable successors of Dupleix were unable to furnish them with a single article necessary for the movement of troops or to give him the smallest information. At length, Lally, driven by the indifference of De Leyrit to extremities, endeavoured to raise funds from the Rájá of Tanjore. The Rájá amused him with promises until Captain Calliaud had sent him some trained sipáhis from Trichinopoli. Then he threw off the mask and bade defiance to the French army. Lally was about to assault the place when a message reached him that the French fleet had been beaten off the coast, and that the English were threatening his base. He returned then to Pondichery without risking an assault, found there three lakhs of rupees which the Admiral had taken from a Dutch vessel which he had plundered, then despatching orders to Bussy to join him, marched to Arcot. Arcot fell without a blow. Bussy joined him from Aurangábád, Moracin with 250 men and 100,000 rupees from the Northern Sirkars; he himself, by returning to Pondichery, wrung some more money from the Pondichery Council; then, taking the strong places which lay between Arcot and Madras, appeared before the latter place on the 12th of December. He had under his orders 2000 European infantry, 300 cavalry, and 5000 trained sipáhis.

Into the details of the siege which followed it is unnecessary to enter. It will suffice to state that although Lally took easy possession of the Black Town, the fort resisted with such resolution that, notwithstanding some advantages gained in the open, one of which he unaccountably failed to press home, he was ultimately compelled to raise the siege. His heavy guns had already made a breach in the fortifications, and he was waiting for a favourable night to order the assault, when the English fleet appeared off the coast. It was the 16th of February. Lally's resources were exhausted. The following day, full of rage and disappointment, he raised the siege.

The most fatal mistake committed by Lally up to this point was the recalling of Bussy and his troops from the Court of the Subáhdár, and of Moracin from the Northern Sirkars. To replace the latter he had sent the Marquis de Conflans, an officer with no Indian experience. The consequences were fatal to French domination. One of the Rájás in the northern part of the Northern Sirkars seized the occasion to assert his independence, and despatched pressing requests to Calcutta for assistance. Clive, thoroughly alive to the possibilities which might result from

English interference, sent his best officer, Colonel Forde, with a small number of troops to aid the Rájá. The consequences justified the action of the great Englishman, taken though it was against[1] the advice of every member of his Council. They were in every way most advantageous to England. Forde, the superior soldier, the man who knew India, pitted against Conflans, the inferior soldier, recently imported from Europe, not only conquered for England the Northern Sirkars, but compelled the Sabáhdár of the Deccan, who interfered at the head of an army to support the French, to transfer his alliance from that people to the English. It is from the period of the expulsion of the French from the Northern Sirkars that date the reciprocal engagements between the Nizám and the Anglo-Indian Government which exist in a modified form to the present day.

Meanwhile Lally, leaving his troops under De Soupire at Arcot, had returned to Pondichery to arrange for means to carry on the war. After many delays and many mischances, he rejoined the army at Wandiwash, and marched with it to Arcot. During his absence, the English force, recently strengthened and now commanded by another of Clive's lieutenants, the renowned Eyre Coote, had taken Wandiwash. Lally marched to recover the place, and took up a strong position before it. There, the 21st of January, 1760, he was attacked and completely defeated by

[1] For a detailed account of these transactions the reader is referred to Malleson's *Decisive Battles of India*, new edition, pp. 77–114.

Eyre Coote. The victory of the English was decisive[1]. 'It dealt a fatal and decisive blow to French domination in India: it shattered to the ground the mighty fabric which Martin, Dumas, and Dupleix had contributed to erect: it dissipated all the hopes of Lally: it sealed the fate of Pondichery.' As an immediate consequence, Arcot, Devikota, Karikál fell into the hands of the English. In September Pondichery was invested. On the 15th of January following it surrendered. Lally, taken prisoner, was sent to England. Learning there that the most shameless charges were preferred against him by the Franco-Indian colony which had thwarted him in India, he asked and obtained permission to return to France to defend himself. But there the influences of the governing clique, always powerful, were too strong. He was condemned on the most casual evidence[1], and after three years of lingering agony was condemned to be beheaded. On May 8, 1766, he was transferred from prison to a dung-cart, and with a gag thrust into his mouth, was taken through the streets of Paris to the scaffold. The Directors of the Company of the Indies had prevailed against him as they had prevailed against Dupleix. It was not till some years later that the incessant exertions of his son, the famous Lally-Tollendal, obtained the rehabilitation of the memory of his father.

But there was yet to be another and a final attempt to restore the policy of Dupleix in Southern India.

[1] Vide *History of the French in India*, p. 560.

The Treaty of Paris, signed February 10, 1763, had restored Pondichery to France, but it was Pondichery dismantled, beggared, bereft of all her influence. During the fifteen years that followed that humiliating treaty, Pondichery had been forced to witness, without attempting to prevent it, the aggrandisement of her rival. Even when, in 1778, the war between France and England was renewed in Europe, the Government of France was ill-prepared to assert a claim for independence, still less for dominion, for her Indian possessions.

The natural results followed. Chandarnagar surrendered without striking a blow (July 10, 1778). Pondichery, ably defended for forty days against vastly superior forces, was captured in the month of September following. The French fleet, commanded by M. de Tronjoly, abandoned the Indian waters without even attempting to save Mahé. All seemed lost; when suddenly the genius of Haidar Alí, the ruler of Mysore, gave a turn to events which upset the most careful calculations, and communicated to his French allies the most brilliant hopes.

On the 4th of April, 1769, Haidar Alí dictated peace to the English under the walls of Madras. By one of the articles of this treaty the contracting parties bound themselves to assist one another in defensive wars. But when, during the following year, Haidar was attacked by the Maráthás, and called upon the English to fulfil their contract, the English refused.

Haidar never forgave this breach of faith. When, some nine years later, he heard of the war between France and England, and noticed that the English were likewise embroiled with the Maráthás in Western India, he took his revenge. Under the pretext that the capture of Mahé was a breach of the treaty existing with him, he declared war, out-manœuvred Sir Hector Munro, destroyed Baillie's detachment of 3720 men (September 9 and 10, 1780), captured Arcot, and seemed to threaten Madras itself.

Haidar had not been unmindful of the advantages which might accrue to him from an alliance with France. Early in the year he had caused information to be sent to Paris of his intentions to crush the English out of Southern India, a result, he said, which would be certain if France would only assist him. But the Ministers of Louis XVI, discouraged by the results of their former attempts in India, and possibly distrusting the power of Haidar Alí, turned a deaf ear to his solicitations, and contented themselves with despatching a squadron to defend the Isles of France and Bourbon. But it soon appeared that such a squadron, if commanded by a man of energy, was sufficient to turn the scale in India.

The squadron, commanded by M. Duchemin, found at Port Louis the officer commanding on the Indian station, the Chevalier d'Orves. D'Orves at once assumed command, and with the six men-of-war, one frigate, and two corvettes, carrying one of the finest regiments in the French army, sailed for the Indian waters. He arrived off the Coromandel coast towards the end of January. I shall now proceed to show how, had he possessed the smallest modicum of sense or energy, had he not been the worst officer who ever commanded a fleet, he might have compelled the surrender of the only available English force in Southern India. It was an opportunity such as Fortune but rarely offers, and which only a fool or a coward refuses.

Haidar Alí, having out-manœuvred Munro, beaten Baillie, and captured Arcot, had laid siege to Wandiwash, Vellore, Ambur, Permakol, and Chengalpat. He had compelled the surrender of Ambur when he heard that Sir Eyre Coote, whom Warren Hastings, with his wonted prescience, had despatched to restore the British fortunes in Southern India, had left Madras the previous day with the intention of attacking him. Haidar, who had the true instinct of a general, at once massed his forces, and so manœuvred as to interpose between Coote and Madras. Coote, careless of this, was bent only on reaching Pondichery, from which place the French had managed to expel the small English garrison. Haidar followed him, carefully occupying the strong places on the way. At length, on the 8th of February, he came close up with the English force near Gudalur, that force being nearest the sea, whilst Haidar, marching almost parallel to it, commanded the country inland. Coote, in fact, was between Haidar and the sea, the strong places in front of him and behind him occupied by his enemies. His supplies were exhausted, but he was expecting these in vessels which had been sent from Madras to Gudalur. Turning on that eventful morning his longing eyes towards the sea to spy, if he could, the expected vessels, Coote saw, and Haidar saw, not the English flag, but the squadron of the Chevalier d'Orves, guarding the coast and cutting off from the English army all chances of supply. Coote, a capable soldier, recognised at once the hopelessness of his position. The only chance of escape was to force Haidar to a battle. He tried every expedient to draw the Asiatic warrior. But Haidar was too wary. He recognised the position as clearly as did Coote, and he was not to be drawn.

Haidar knew, in fact, that, barring accidents, Coote must surrender. He therefore communicated with D'Orves, and begged him to land the regiment he had with him, pointing out to him that the only army possessed by England in Southern India was at his mercy, and that Madras was garrisoned by but five hundred invalids.

Never had France such an opportunity. It was an absolute certainty. There was neither risk nor chance about it. The English fleet under Sir Edward Hughes was off the western coast. D'Orves had but to remain quietly where he was for a few days and the English force must be starved into surrender. Sir Eyre Coote saw it, Haidar Alí saw it, every man in the army saw it: every man with the squadron, one only excepted, saw it. The exception was D'Orves himself. But little was required of him. He, the representative of France on the Indian seas, had but to ride at anchor where he was in the finest season of the year, a season when storms are unknown in the Indian seas, and watch the enemies of his country surrender or starve —and he would not. Despite the protestations of Haidar and the murmurs of his crews, D'Orves sailed for the islands the 15th of February, taking every man he had brought with him. His departure saved Coote. A few days later English vessels arrived with provisions from Madras.

Haidar, thus left to himself, fought Coote on the 1st July at Chilambaram, and, after a hardly contested battle, was beaten. On the 27th August following, he engaged the English general at Parambákam, and this time not unequally. He left, however, to Coote the honour of the field of battle. On the 18th of February following (1782), Típu Sáhib, the eldest son of Haidar, compelled Colonel Braithwaite's detachment, after three days' hard fighting, to surrender. It was about the period of this last encounter that France made her third and last effort to take up the dropped policy of Dupleix. She despatched to the Indian seas a powerful squadron under the greatest of her admirals, the illustrious Suffren, and nearly 3000 men under Bussy. Pending the arrival of Bussy, the land force was placed under the orders of the Duchemin already mentioned.

Leaving Suffren and the English admiral, Sir Edward Hughes, to fight four or five indecisive battles off the Coromandel coast, I propose to follow very briefly the fortunes of Duchemin. It was just a chance that at this decisive period, pending the arrival of the real commander, the charge of the French troops should have devolved on a man who dreaded nothing so much as responsibility. Had a real soldier commanded that force—and there was one there serving in the ranks, the Bernadotte who afterwards became a Marshal of France and King of Sweden—the fate of Southern India would for a time have been changed.

Duchemin and his troops had disembarked at Porto Novo the 20th of April. It had been arranged between Suffren and Haidar that a corps of 6000 native infantry and 4000 cavalry from the Mysore army should join the French force, form with it an army-corps, and as such, should, under Duchemin's orders, co-operate with Haidar's main army, the latter furnishing it with money and supplies. This arrangement took effect, and Duchemin, after re-taking Gudalur, joined Haidar at Permakol, whence they marched to take a position before Wandiwash.

The English force, still commanded by Coote, consisted of 12,000 men, of whom only 2000 were Europeans. Coote himself was in feeble health, but his spirit, always daring, was as resolute as it was on the day when he voted against Clive to fight at Plassey.

His situation was a dangerous one. Before him was an army of 60,000 men, led by the best native general who has ever been seen in India, backed by a corps of upwards of 2000 Frenchmen. It seemed probable that before that force Wandiwash must fall. Now it was everything to Coote to prevent the fall of Wandiwash. He marched, then, with his inferior force, and offered battle to Haidar and Duchemin. It was a daring, even a rash offer. He was over-matched in the three arms, and, considering the enormously preponderating numbers of the enemy's cavalry, defeat would have been ruin. Haidar saw the advantage, and pressed upon Duchemin to prepare his men for battle. The very reasons which made it rash to Coote to offer battle incited Haidar, and should have incited Duchemin, to accept it. But the responsibility weighed down Duchemin to the earth. He was only acting-commander, for Bussy had not arrived: and he had not the nerve to accept the gift which a too kind Fortune placed within his reach. Haidar, disgusted with his ally, fell back on Kalinur, near Pondichery. Watching thence the operations of Coote, he learned that the English General was about to attempt Ární. In Ární he had stored his magazines and ammunition. On no account must Ární be lost. Leaving then Duchemin and his corps behind him, he proceeded by forced marches to intercept Coote; caught him, and though he failed to defeat him, baffled his design on Ární. Four days later he enticed a detachment of Coote's army into an ambuscade, and cut it up. Coote then retired on Madras, and Haidar laid siege to Vellore.

Before Bussy could reach India, Haidar had died.

When at last, March 19, Bussy did arrive, it was soon recognised that he was not the same Bussy who had won and had maintained for many years a commanding position at the Court of the Subáhdár of the Deccan. The Bussy who landed in Gudalur in March, 1783, was a gouty gourmand who would undertake nothing and sanction nothing. He remained invisible in his tent, whilst he allowed an English army, inferior in the number of its Europeans, to blockade him in Gudalur. He was in this position when the news arrived that peace between England and France had been signed. The moment was fortunate for the English commander. Suffren had just driven the English squadron from the coast: the supplies in the English camp were exhausted. Had Bussy declined to accede to an armistice, the English army must have surrendered [1].

But it was not to be. Bussy accepted the armistice with alacrity, and the Peace of Versailles soon after formally put an end to the war.

Since that period France has renounced all open attempts to found a French Empire in India. For nearly twenty years later, by permitting her children to enlist in the service of native princes, to discipline their armies and to show them how to occupy

[1] Professor H. H. Wilson writes on this subject: 'It seems probable that but for the opportune occurrence of peace with France the South of India would have been lost to the English.' For a detailed account of the proceedings at this period *vide* the author's *Final French Struggles in India and on the Indian Seas*. W. H. Allen and Co.

defensive positions, she continued to foster the feeling of hostility which Dupleix had been the first to inspire. Within that period also she lured the ruler of Mysore to those open demonstrations against England which the genius of Marquess Wellesley turned to his destruction. But not even when she stood alone against the combined force of Napoleon and his allies, did the ruler of France dare openly to attack the Empire, the conception of which had originated in the brain of Dupleix, but which Clive, Warren Hastings, and Wellesley had gained for England. That the conception was the conception of Dupleix cannot be denied. It was with him a well-thought-out calculation, an organised scheme, an end to be attained by patient striving. It was long before the English regarded it in that aspect. Contented with having defeated the plans of Dupleix they were ready to fall back upon their rôle of merchants. The quasi-imperial idea came to Clive only when he recognised that unless the English should crush Surâju-d-daulah, Surâju-d-daulah would crush the English. But how far, even after his victory, even after the annexation of Bengal and Behar, Clive was from having adopted the entire programme of Dupleix, was shown by the earnest injunctions he laid upon his successor not to advance the frontier beyond the point at which he had left it[1]. Action of the same

[1] 'Our possessions should be bounded by the provinces (Bengal and Behar). Studiously maintain peace, it is the groundwork of our prosperity. Never consent to act offensively against any Powers,

character as that which had forced the hand of Clive, forced subsequently the hand of Warren Hastings; and later still, the hand of Wellesley. Vainly did Cornwallis, and Teignmouth, and Adam, and Minto try to stop the inevitable march forward. Such a march was the certain ultimate consequence of the establishment of a factory on the Húglí by a dominant race. There was no middle point between crushing or being crushed. The possibility of succeeding in the former process was first demonstrated by Dupleix, when he declined to surrender Madras to the Nuwáb of the Karnátik. The defeat his general inflicted upon the Nuwáb's troops on the Adyár, not only reversed the moral position of the European and the Asiatic in India, but it revealed to his soaring and receptive mind the possibility of bringing the whole of Southern India under French domination. Had France but seconded him, who can say that his dream might not have been realised? It remains only to us, whilst concluding this record of his splendid struggles to that end, and his glorious and unmerited failure, to admit to the full the contention of M. Xavier Raymond, which, though already quoted, may well bear repetition. 'England has been much

except in defence of our own, the King's (of Delhí), or the Nuwáb-Wazir's dominions, as stipulated by treaty; and, above all things, be assured that a march to Delhi would be not only a vain and fruitless project, but attended with destruction to your own army, and perhaps put a period to the very being of the Company in Bengal.' Minute of Lord Clive, given in extenso by Mr. Talboys Wheeler in his *Early Records of British India.*

admired and often cited for having resolved that great problem of how to govern, at a distance of 4000 leagues, with some hundreds of civil functionaries and some thousands of soldiers, her immense possessions in India. If there is much that is wonderful, much that is bold and daring, much political genius in the idea, it must be admitted that the honour of inaugurating it belonged to Dupleix, and that England, which is reaping the profit and the glory, has had but to follow the path which the Genius of France opened out to her.'

INDEX

THE END.